Architecture Competency
Complete Self-Assessment Guide

The guidance in this Self-Assessment is based on Architecture Competency best practices and standards in business process architecture, design and quality management. The guidance is also based on the professional judgment of the individual collaborators listed in the Acknowledgments.

Notice of rights

Table of Contents

About The Art of Service

The Art of Service, Business Process Architects since 2000, is dedicated to helping stakeholders achieve excellence.

Defining, designing, creating, and implementing a process to solve a stakeholders challenge or meet an objective is the most valuable role… In EVERY group, company, organization and department.

Unless you're talking a one-time, single-use project, there should be a process. Whether that process is managed and implemented by humans, AI, or a combination of the two, it needs to be designed by someone with a complex enough perspective to ask the right questions.

Someone capable of asking the right questions and step back and say, 'What are we really trying to accomplish here? And is there a different way to look at it?'

With The Art of Service's Standard Requirements Self-Assessments, we empower people who can do just that — whether their title is marketer, entrepreneur, manager, salesperson, consultant, Business Process Manager, executive assistant, IT Manager, CIO etc... —they are the people who rule the future. They are people who watch the process as it happens, and ask the right questions to make the process work better.

Contact us when you need any support with this Self-Assessment and any help with templates, blue-prints and examples of standard documents you might need:

http://theartofservice.com
service@theartofservice.com

Included Resources - how to access

Included with your purchase of the book is the Architecture

Competency Self-Assessment Spreadsheet Dashboard which contains all questions and Self-Assessment areas and auto-generates insights, graphs, and project RACI planning - all with examples to get you started right away.

How? Simply send an email to
access@theartofservice.com
with this books' title in the subject to get the Architecture Competency Self Assessment Tool right away.

You will receive the following contents with New and Updated specific criteria:

- The latest quick edition of the book in PDF

- The latest complete edition of the book in PDF, which criteria correspond to the criteria in...

- The Self-Assessment Excel Dashboard, and...

- Example pre-filled Self-Assessment Excel Dashboard to get familiar with results generation

- In-depth specific Checklists covering the topic

- Project management checklists and templates to assist with implementation

Purpose of this Self-Assessment

This Self-Assessment has been developed to improve understanding of the requirements and elements of Architecture Competency, based on best practices and standards in business process architecture, design and quality management.

It is designed to allow for a rapid Self-Assessment to determine how closely existing management practices and procedures correspond to the elements of the Self-Assessment.

The criteria of requirements and elements of Architecture Competency have been rephrased in the format of a Self-Assessment questionnaire, with a seven-criterion scoring system, as explained in this document.

In this format, even with limited background knowledge of Architecture Competency, a manager can quickly review existing operations to determine how they measure up to the standards. This in turn can serve as the starting point of a 'gap analysis' to identify management tools or system elements that might usefully be implemented in the organization to help improve overall performance.

How to use the Self-Assessment

On the following pages are a series of questions to identify to what extent your Architecture Competency initiative is complete in comparison to the requirements set in standards.

To facilitate answering the questions, there is a space in front of each question to enter a score on a scale of '1' to '5'.

1 Strongly Disagree

2 Disagree

3 Neutral

4 Agree

5 Strongly Agree

Read the question and rate it with the following in front of mind:

'In my belief, the answer to this question is clearly defined'.

There are two ways in which you can choose to interpret this statement;
1. how aware are you that the answer to the question is clearly defined
2. for more in-depth analysis you can choose to gather evidence and confirm the answer to the question. This obviously will take more time, most Self-Assessment users opt for the first way to interpret the question and dig deeper later on based on the outcome of the overall Self-Assessment.

A score of '1' would mean that the answer is not clear at all, where a '5' would mean the answer is crystal clear and defined. Leave emtpy when the question is not applicable or you don't want to answer it, you can skip it without affecting your score. Write your score in the space provided.

After you have responded to all the appropriate statements in each section, compute your average score for that section, using the formula provided, and round to the nearest tenth. Then transfer to the corresponding spoke in the Architecture Competency Scorecard on the second next page of the Self-Assessment.

Your completed Architecture Competency Scorecard will give you a clear presentation of which Architecture Competency areas need attention.

Architecture Competency
Scorecard Example

Example of how the finalized Scorecard can look like:

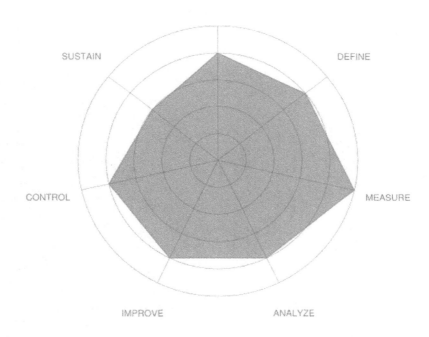

Architecture Competency Scorecard

Your Scores:

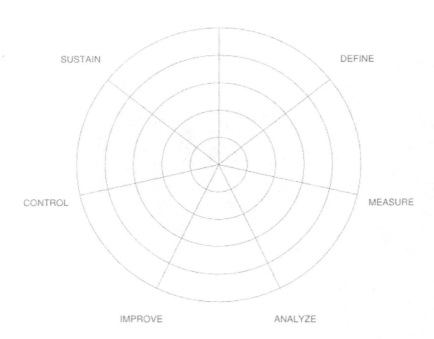

BEGINNING OF THE SELF-ASSESSMENT:

CRITERION #1: RECOGNIZE

INTENT: Be aware of the need for change. Recognize that there is an unfavorable variation, problem or symptom.

In my belief, the answer to this question is clearly defined:

5 Strongly Agree

4 Agree

3 Neutral

2 Disagree

1 Strongly Disagree

1. Are you dealing with any of the same issues today as yesterday? What can you do about this?
<--- Score

2. Have you identified your architecture competency key performance indicators?
<--- Score

3. How are training requirements identified?

<--- Score

4. What prevents you from making the changes you know will make you a more effective architecture competency leader?
<--- Score

5. What needs to stay?
<--- Score

6. Which needs are not included or involved?
<--- Score

7. As a sponsor, customer or management, how important is it to meet goals, objectives?
<--- Score

8. What should be considered when identifying available resources, constraints, and deadlines?
<--- Score

9. Does the problem have ethical dimensions?
<--- Score

10. What needs to be done?
<--- Score

11. Do you recognize architecture competency achievements?
<--- Score

12. What are your needs in relation to architecture competency skills, labor, equipment, and markets?
<--- Score

13. To what extent does each concerned units

management team recognize architecture competency as an effective investment?
<--- Score

14. What is the recognized need?
<--- Score

15. Are problem definition and motivation clearly presented?
<--- Score

16. What tools and technologies are needed for a custom architecture competency project?
<--- Score

17. What is the problem and/or vulnerability?
<--- Score

18. Consider your own architecture competency project, what types of organizational problems do you think might be causing or affecting your problem, based on the work done so far?
<--- Score

19. Is the quality assurance team identified?
<--- Score

20. Are there any specific expectations or concerns about the architecture competency team, architecture competency itself?
<--- Score

21. What extra resources will you need?
<--- Score

22. For your architecture competency project, identify

and describe the business environment, is there more than one layer to the business environment?
<--- Score

23. Will it solve real problems?
<--- Score

24. Who needs budgets?
<--- Score

25. Are there any revenue recognition issues?
<--- Score

26. How much are sponsors, customers, partners, stakeholders involved in architecture competency? In other words, what are the risks, if architecture competency does not deliver successfully?
<--- Score

27. What information do users need?
<--- Score

28. Where is training needed?
<--- Score

29. How many trainings, in total, are needed?
<--- Score

30. Are losses recognized in a timely manner?
<--- Score

31. How are the architecture competency's objectives aligned to the group's overall stakeholder strategy?
<--- Score

32. How does it fit into your organizational needs and

tasks?
<--- Score

33. Do you have/need 24-hour access to key personnel?
<--- Score

34. What is the smallest subset of the problem you can usefully solve?
<--- Score

35. How do you recognize an objection?
<--- Score

36. How can auditing be a preventative security measure?
<--- Score

37. What are the stakeholder objectives to be achieved with architecture competency?
<--- Score

38. Can management personnel recognize the monetary benefit of architecture competency?
<--- Score

39. Who are your key stakeholders who need to sign off?
<--- Score

40. How do you identify the kinds of information that you will need?
<--- Score

41. What else needs to be measured?
<--- Score

42. Who needs to know?
<--- Score

43. Who defines the rules in relation to any given issue?
<--- Score

44. How do you take a forward-looking perspective in identifying architecture competency research related to market response and models?
<--- Score

45. Would you recognize a threat from the inside?
<--- Score

46. What are the expected benefits of architecture competency to the stakeholder?
<--- Score

47. What vendors make products that address the architecture competency needs?
<--- Score

48. What architecture competency coordination do you need?
<--- Score

49. What are the minority interests and what amount of minority interests can be recognized?
<--- Score

50. What architecture competency capabilities do you need?
<--- Score

51. Why the need?
<--- Score

52. What creative shifts do you need to take?
<--- Score

53. What does architecture competency success mean to the stakeholders?
<--- Score

54. When a architecture competency manager recognizes a problem, what options are available?
<--- Score

55. Do you need to avoid or amend any architecture competency activities?
<--- Score

56. Are employees recognized or rewarded for performance that demonstrates the highest levels of integrity?
<--- Score

57. Which issues are too important to ignore?
<--- Score

58. How do you identify subcontractor relationships?
<--- Score

59. Does your organization need more architecture competency education?
<--- Score

60. Why is this needed?
<--- Score

61. Will new equipment/products be required to facilitate architecture competency delivery, for example is new software needed?
<--- Score

62. Will a response program recognize when a crisis occurs and provide some level of response?
<--- Score

63. Think about the people you identified for your architecture competency project and the project responsibilities you would assign to them, what kind of training do you think they would need to perform these responsibilities effectively?
<--- Score

64. What are the timeframes required to resolve each of the issues/problems?
<--- Score

65. What architecture competency problem should be solved?
<--- Score

66. Are controls defined to recognize and contain problems?
<--- Score

67. Does architecture competency create potential expectations in other areas that need to be recognized and considered?
<--- Score

68. Which information does the architecture competency business case need to include?
<--- Score

69. To what extent would your organization benefit from being recognized as a award recipient?
<--- Score

70. Who needs to know about architecture competency?
<--- Score

71. Do you need different information or graphics?
<--- Score

72. What do you need to start doing?
<--- Score

73. Did you miss any major architecture competency issues?
<--- Score

74. How are you going to measure success?
<--- Score

75. Are employees recognized for desired behaviors?
<--- Score

76. Whom do you really need or want to serve?
<--- Score

77. Who should resolve the architecture competency issues?
<--- Score

78. What training and capacity building actions are needed to implement proposed reforms?
<--- Score

79. Looking at each person individually – does every one have the qualities which are needed to work in this group?

<--- Score

80. Are there architecture competency problems defined?

<--- Score

81. Is the need for organizational change recognized?

<--- Score

82. What problems are you facing and how do you consider architecture competency will circumvent those obstacles?

<--- Score

83. Where do you need to exercise leadership?

<--- Score

84. How do you assess your architecture competency workforce capability and capacity needs, including skills, competencies, and staffing levels?

<--- Score

85. What do employees need in the short term?

<--- Score

86. What resources or support might you need?

<--- Score

87. Are there regulatory / compliance issues?

<--- Score

88. How do you recognize an architecture competency objection?
<--- Score

89. What is the architecture competency problem definition? What do you need to resolve?
<--- Score

90. What would happen if architecture competency weren't done?
<--- Score

91. Will architecture competency deliverables need to be tested and, if so, by whom?
<--- Score

92. Are there recognized architecture competency problems?
<--- Score

93. What situation(s) led to this architecture competency Self Assessment?
<--- Score

94. What activities does the governance board need to consider?
<--- Score

95. What are the architecture competency resources needed?
<--- Score

96. Who else hopes to benefit from it?
<--- Score

97. Is it needed?

<--- Score

Add up total points for this section:
_____ = Total points for this section

Divided by: _____ (number of
statements answered) = _____
Average score for this section

Transfer your score to the architecture
competency Index at the beginning of
the Self-Assessment.

CRITERION #2: DEFINE:

INTENT: Formulate the stakeholder problem. Define the problem, needs and objectives.

In my belief, the answer to this question is clearly defined:

5 Strongly Agree

4 Agree

3 Neutral

2 Disagree

1 Strongly Disagree

1. Is architecture competency required?
<--- Score

2. Who is gathering architecture competency information?
<--- Score

3. Do you have organizational privacy requirements?

<--- Score

4. Is there a completed, verified, and validated high-level 'as is' (not 'should be' or 'could be') stakeholder process map?
<--- Score

5. What sources do you use to gather information for a architecture competency study?
<--- Score

6. Are accountability and ownership for architecture competency clearly defined?
<--- Score

7. Are there different segments of customers?
<--- Score

8. Are the architecture competency requirements complete?
<--- Score

9. Has a project plan, Gantt chart, or similar been developed/completed?
<--- Score

10. Is there regularly 100% attendance at the team meetings? If not, have appointed substitutes attended to preserve cross-functionality and full representation?
<--- Score

11. Is the architecture competency scope manageable?
<--- Score

12. When is the estimated completion date?
<--- Score

13. Are there any constraints known that bear on the ability to perform architecture competency work? How is the team addressing them?
<--- Score

14. What is a worst-case scenario for losses?
<--- Score

15. How and when will the baselines be defined?
<--- Score

16. How do you build the right business case?
<--- Score

17. What are the dynamics of the communication plan?
<--- Score

18. Are all requirements met?
<--- Score

19. What are the record-keeping requirements of architecture competency activities?
<--- Score

20. Are task requirements clearly defined?
<--- Score

21. The political context: who holds power?
<--- Score

22. What specifically is the problem? Where does it occur? When does it occur? What is its extent?

<--- Score

23. Are resources adequate for the scope?
<--- Score

24. How do you manage changes in architecture competency requirements?
<--- Score

25. Does the team have regular meetings?
<--- Score

26. Are the architecture competency requirements testable?
<--- Score

27. Has a architecture competency requirement not been met?
<--- Score

28. How was the 'as is' process map developed, reviewed, verified and validated?
<--- Score

29. What critical content must be communicated – who, what, when, where, and how?
<--- Score

30. What information do you gather?
<--- Score

31. How do you manage scope?
<--- Score

32. What are (control) requirements for architecture competency Information?

<--- Score

33. Has a team charter been developed and communicated?
<--- Score

34. What is the definition of architecture competency excellence?
<--- Score

35. Do you all define architecture competency in the same way?
<--- Score

36. How do you gather the stories?
<--- Score

37. What are the rough order estimates on cost savings/opportunities that architecture competency brings?
<--- Score

38. Has the architecture competency work been fairly and/or equitably divided and delegated among team members who are qualified and capable to perform the work? Has everyone contributed?
<--- Score

39. Is the improvement team aware of the different versions of a process: what they think it is vs. what it actually is vs. what it should be vs. what it could be?
<--- Score

40. Has the improvement team collected the 'voice of the customer' (obtained feedback – qualitative and quantitative)?

<--- Score

41. What system do you use for gathering architecture competency information?
<--- Score

42. What is the scope of the architecture competency work?
<--- Score

43. Are audit criteria, scope, frequency and methods defined?
<--- Score

44. What sort of initial information to gather?
<--- Score

45. What are the boundaries of the scope? What is in bounds and what is not? What is the start point? What is the stop point?
<--- Score

46. Who defines (or who defined) the rules and roles?
<--- Score

47. How do you gather architecture competency requirements?
<--- Score

48. How do you think the partners involved in architecture competency would have defined success?
<--- Score

49. Are approval levels defined for contracts and supplements to contracts?

<--- Score

50. Are roles and responsibilities formally defined?
<--- Score

51. Have specific policy objectives been defined?
<--- Score

52. In what way can you redefine the criteria of choice clients have in your category in your favor?
<--- Score

53. Does the scope remain the same?
<--- Score

54. What was the context?
<--- Score

55. Is the scope of architecture competency defined?
<--- Score

56. Is scope creep really all bad news?
<--- Score

57. What is the scope of architecture competency?
<--- Score

58. What architecture competency requirements should be gathered?
<--- Score

59. What is the definition of success?
<--- Score

60. What is out-of-scope initially?

<--- Score

61. Scope of sensitive information?
<--- Score

62. What is the context?
<--- Score

63. What customer feedback methods were used to solicit their input?
<--- Score

64. Is the work to date meeting requirements?
<--- Score

65. Is the current 'as is' process being followed? If not, what are the discrepancies?
<--- Score

66. If substitutes have been appointed, have they been briefed on the architecture competency goals and received regular communications as to the progress to date?
<--- Score

67. How will the architecture competency team and the group measure complete success of architecture competency?
<--- Score

68. What are the architecture competency use cases?
<--- Score

69. When are meeting minutes sent out? Who is on the distribution list?
<--- Score

70. How have you defined all architecture competency requirements first?
<--- Score

71. Has anyone else (internal or external to the group) attempted to solve this problem or a similar one before? If so, what knowledge can be leveraged from these previous efforts?
<--- Score

72. How would you define architecture competency leadership?
<--- Score

73. Why are you doing architecture competency and what is the scope?
<--- Score

74. Is it clearly defined in and to your organization what you do?
<--- Score

75. What baselines are required to be defined and managed?
<--- Score

76. What information should you gather?
<--- Score

77. What defines best in class?
<--- Score

78. What key stakeholder process output measure(s) does architecture competency leverage and how?
<--- Score

79. What are the Roles and Responsibilities for each team member and its leadership? Where is this documented?
<--- Score

80. Has the direction changed at all during the course of architecture competency? If so, when did it change and why?
<--- Score

81. Who approved the architecture competency scope?
<--- Score

82. Have the customer needs been translated into specific, measurable requirements? How?
<--- Score

83. What constraints exist that might impact the team?
<--- Score

84. What is the worst case scenario?
<--- Score

85. Who are the architecture competency improvement team members, including Management Leads and Coaches?
<--- Score

86. Will a architecture competency production readiness review be required?
<--- Score

87. Is architecture competency linked to key

stakeholder goals and objectives?
<--- Score

88. How do you gather requirements?
<--- Score

89. What is out of scope?
<--- Score

90. How would you define the culture at your organization, how susceptible is it to architecture competency changes?
<--- Score

91. Have all basic functions of architecture competency been defined?
<--- Score

92. How do you hand over architecture competency context?
<--- Score

93. What happens if architecture competency's scope changes?
<--- Score

94. What intelligence can you gather?
<--- Score

95. When is/was the architecture competency start date?
<--- Score

96. Has your scope been defined?
<--- Score

97. What are the compelling stakeholder reasons for embarking on architecture competency?
<--- Score

98. Is there a architecture competency management charter, including stakeholder case, problem and goal statements, scope, milestones, roles and responsibilities, communication plan?
<--- Score

99. How did the architecture competency manager receive input to the development of a architecture competency improvement plan and the estimated completion dates/times of each activity?
<--- Score

100. Is there any additional architecture competency definition of success?
<--- Score

101. How do you keep key subject matter experts in the loop?
<--- Score

102. How do you catch architecture competency definition inconsistencies?
<--- Score

103. Do the problem and goal statements meet the SMART criteria (specific, measurable, attainable, relevant, and time-bound)?
<--- Score

104. Has a high-level 'as is' process map been completed, verified and validated?
<--- Score

105. How do you manage unclear architecture competency requirements?
<--- Score

106. Has/have the customer(s) been identified?
<--- Score

107. How often are the team meetings?
<--- Score

108. Is there a completed SIPOC representation, describing the Suppliers, Inputs, Process, Outputs, and Customers?
<--- Score

109. What scope do you want your strategy to cover?
<--- Score

110. What architecture competency services do you require?
<--- Score

111. How does the architecture competency manager ensure against scope creep?
<--- Score

112. What scope to assess?
<--- Score

113. Is there a critical path to deliver architecture competency results?
<--- Score

114. How is the team tracking and documenting its work?

<--- Score

115. How are consistent architecture competency definitions important?
<--- Score

116. Is special architecture competency user knowledge required?
<--- Score

117. What knowledge or experience is required?
<--- Score

118. Is there a clear architecture competency case definition?
<--- Score

119. Is the team adequately staffed with the desired cross-functionality? If not, what additional resources are available to the team?
<--- Score

120. What gets examined?
<--- Score

121. What is the scope of the architecture competency effort?
<--- Score

122. Has everyone on the team, including the team leaders, been properly trained?
<--- Score

123. Are different versions of process maps needed to account for the different types of inputs?
<--- Score

124. Is architecture competency currently on schedule according to the plan?
<--- Score

125. What is the scope?
<--- Score

126. What are the core elements of the architecture competency business case?
<--- Score

127. What are the requirements for audit information?
<--- Score

128. How will variation in the actual durations of each activity be dealt with to ensure that the expected architecture competency results are met?
<--- Score

129. What would be the goal or target for a architecture competency's improvement team?
<--- Score

130. Who is gathering information?
<--- Score

131. What are the architecture competency tasks and definitions?
<--- Score

132. Are required metrics defined, what are they?
<--- Score

133. Do you have a architecture competency success

story or case study ready to tell and share?
<--- Score

134. How can the value of architecture competency be defined?
<--- Score

Add up total points for this section:
_ _ _ _ _ = Total points for this section

Divided by: _ _ _ _ _ _ (number of statements answered) = _ _ _ _ _ _
Average score for this section

Transfer your score to the architecture competency Index at the beginning of the Self-Assessment.

CRITERION #3: MEASURE:

In my belief, the answer to this
question is clearly defined:

5 Strongly Agree

4 Agree

3 Neutral

2 Disagree

1 Strongly Disagree

1. What relevant entities could be measured?
<--- Score

2. What are your customers expectations and measures?
<--- Score

3. What details are required of the architecture competency cost structure?

<--- Score

4. What is the total fixed cost?
<--- Score

5. Are the units of measure consistent?
<--- Score

6. How will your organization measure success?
<--- Score

7. Was a business case (cost/benefit) developed?
<--- Score

8. What could cause delays in the schedule?
<--- Score

9. What tests verify requirements?
<--- Score

10. What do people want to verify?
<--- Score

11. What is the cost of rework?
<--- Score

12. When are costs are incurred?
<--- Score

13. What are the costs and benefits?
<--- Score

14. How will effects be measured?
<--- Score

15. How do you focus on what is right -not who is

right?
<--- Score

16. What evidence is there and what is measured?
<--- Score

17. How do you verify your resources?
<--- Score

18. What are the costs of reform?
<--- Score

19. What drives O&M cost?
<--- Score

20. Which architecture competency impacts are significant?
<--- Score

21. Are you aware of what could cause a problem?
<--- Score

22. Who pays the cost?
<--- Score

23. What would be a real cause for concern?
<--- Score

24. Are supply costs steady or fluctuating?
<--- Score

25. How long to keep data and how to manage retention costs?
<--- Score

26. What is measured? Why?

<--- Score

27. How do you measure variability?
<--- Score

28. How do you control the overall costs of your work processes?
<--- Score

29. How can you reduce the costs of obtaining inputs?
<--- Score

30. What is the total cost related to deploying architecture competency, including any consulting or professional services?
<--- Score

31. What causes investor action?
<--- Score

32. What are the current costs of the architecture competency process?
<--- Score

33. What users will be impacted?
<--- Score

34. Are there measurements based on task performance?
<--- Score

35. Are missed architecture competency opportunities costing your organization money?
<--- Score

36. What are the strategic priorities for this year?
<--- Score

37. Who is involved in verifying compliance?
<--- Score

38. Are architecture competency vulnerabilities categorized and prioritized?
<--- Score

39. What do you measure and why?
<--- Score

40. How is performance measured?
<--- Score

41. How do you measure lifecycle phases?
<--- Score

42. What disadvantage does this cause for the user?
<--- Score

43. What does a Test Case verify?
<--- Score

44. What would it cost to replace your technology?
<--- Score

45. Why do you expend time and effort to implement measurement, for whom?
<--- Score

46. Are actual costs in line with budgeted costs?
<--- Score

47. What are your primary costs, revenues, assets?

<--- Score

48. Which measures and indicators matter?
<--- Score

49. Do you effectively measure and reward individual and team performance?
<--- Score

50. What does losing customers cost your organization?
<--- Score

51. How do you verify architecture competency completeness and accuracy?
<--- Score

52. What measurements are being captured?
<--- Score

53. Do you verify that corrective actions were taken?
<--- Score

54. What happens if cost savings do not materialize?
<--- Score

55. How will costs be allocated?
<--- Score

56. Where can you go to verify the info?
<--- Score

57. How do you verify if architecture competency is built right?
<--- Score

58. Among the architecture competency product and service cost to be estimated, which is considered hardest to estimate?
<--- Score

59. Where is the cost?
<--- Score

60. What methods are feasible and acceptable to estimate the impact of reforms?
<--- Score

61. How will measures be used to manage and adapt?
<--- Score

62. How do you verify the authenticity of the data and information used?
<--- Score

63. Do you have a flow diagram of what happens?
<--- Score

64. Is the cost worth the architecture competency effort ?
<--- Score

65. Is it possible to estimate the impact of unanticipated complexity such as wrong or failed assumptions, feedback, etcetera on proposed reforms?
<--- Score

66. Have design-to-cost goals been established?
<--- Score

67. How can a architecture competency test verify your ideas or assumptions?
<--- Score

68. Are the architecture competency benefits worth its costs?
<--- Score

69. How do you prevent mis-estimating cost?
<--- Score

70. What are the architecture competency investment costs?
<--- Score

71. What measurements are possible, practicable and meaningful?
<--- Score

72. How can you measure the performance?
<--- Score

73. Are you able to realize any cost savings?
<--- Score

74. What are you verifying?
<--- Score

75. Are there any easy-to-implement alternatives to architecture competency? Sometimes other solutions are available that do not require the cost implications of a full-blown project?
<--- Score

76. Do you aggressively reward and promote the people who have the biggest impact on creating

excellent architecture competency services/ products?
<--- Score

77. Has a cost center been established?
<--- Score

78. Have you included everything in your architecture competency cost models?
<--- Score

79. Have you made assumptions about the shape of the future, particularly its impact on your customers and competitors?
<--- Score

80. What causes extra work or rework?
<--- Score

81. What could cause you to change course?
<--- Score

82. How do you aggregate measures across priorities?
<--- Score

83. Which costs should be taken into account?
<--- Score

84. What are the costs of delaying architecture competency action?
<--- Score

85. How do you verify performance?
<--- Score

86. What causes innovation to fail or succeed in your

organization?
<--- Score

87. What potential environmental factors impact the architecture competency effort?
<--- Score

88. What causes mismanagement?
<--- Score

89. Do you have any cost architecture competency limitation requirements?
<--- Score

90. What is your decision requirements diagram?
<--- Score

91. Are indirect costs charged to the architecture competency program?
<--- Score

92. Does the architecture competency task fit the client's priorities?
<--- Score

93. What is the architecture competency business impact?
<--- Score

94. How do you verify and validate the architecture competency data?
<--- Score

95. What are the operational costs after architecture competency deployment?
<--- Score

96. Where is it measured?
<--- Score

97. What are the architecture competency key cost drivers?
<--- Score

98. What are allowable costs?
<--- Score

99. Who should receive measurement reports?
<--- Score

100. Do you have an issue in getting priority?
<--- Score

101. What are the estimated costs of proposed changes?
<--- Score

102. How are you verifying it?
<--- Score

103. Is the solution cost-effective?
<--- Score

104. How sensitive must the architecture competency strategy be to cost?
<--- Score

105. At what cost?
<--- Score

106. When a disaster occurs, who gets priority?
<--- Score

107. Why a architecture competency focus?
<--- Score

108. How do you measure success?
<--- Score

109. How much does it cost?
<--- Score

110. How frequently do you track architecture competency measures?
<--- Score

111. How do you verify and develop ideas and innovations?
<--- Score

112. What is your architecture competency quality cost segregation study?
<--- Score

113. What is an unallowable cost?
<--- Score

114. How to cause the change?
<--- Score

115. How can you manage cost down?
<--- Score

116. What are the costs?
<--- Score

117. Why do the measurements/indicators matter?
<--- Score

118. How will you measure success?
<--- Score

119. The approach of traditional architecture competency works for detail complexity but is focused on a systematic approach rather than an understanding of the nature of systems themselves, what approach will permit your organization to deal with the kind of unpredictable emergent behaviors that dynamic complexity can introduce?
<--- Score

120. How do you measure efficient delivery of architecture competency services?
<--- Score

121. What does verifying compliance entail?
<--- Score

122. How do your measurements capture actionable architecture competency information for use in exceeding your customers expectations and securing your customers engagement?
<--- Score

123. Are the measurements objective?
<--- Score

124. How are measurements made?
<--- Score

125. Did you tackle the cause or the symptom?
<--- Score

126. What are the uncertainties surrounding estimates of impact?
<--- Score

127. What are the types and number of measures to use?
<--- Score

128. What is the root cause(s) of the problem?
<--- Score

129. How are costs allocated?
<--- Score

130. When should you bother with diagrams?
<--- Score

131. Do the benefits outweigh the costs?
<--- Score

132. How do you verify the architecture competency requirements quality?
<--- Score

133. How is progress measured?
<--- Score

134. How will success or failure be measured?
<--- Score

135. How is the value delivered by architecture competency being measured?
<--- Score

136. Are you taking your company in the direction of better and revenue or cheaper and cost?

<--- Score

137. What are your operating costs?
<--- Score

138. How can you measure architecture competency in a systematic way?
<--- Score

Add up total points for this section:
_ _ _ _ _ = Total points for this section

Divided by: _ _ _ _ _ _ (number of
statements answered) = _ _ _ _ _ _
Average score for this section

Transfer your score to the architecture
competency Index at the beginning of
the Self-Assessment.

CRITERION #4: ANALYZE:

INTENT: Analyze causes, assumptions and hypotheses.

In my belief, the answer to this question is clearly defined:

5 Strongly Agree

4 Agree

3 Neutral

2 Disagree

1 Strongly Disagree

1. What data do you need to collect?
<--- Score

2. Do your contracts/agreements contain data security obligations?
<--- Score

3. What tools were used to narrow the list of possible causes?
<--- Score

4. What are your best practices for minimizing architecture competency project risk, while demonstrating incremental value and quick wins throughout the architecture competency project lifecycle?
<--- Score

5. What are your current levels and trends in key measures or indicators of architecture competency product and process performance that are important to and directly serve your customers? How do these results compare with the performance of your competitors and other organizations with similar offerings?
<--- Score

6. Is there an established change management process?
<--- Score

7. What are the personnel training and qualifications required?
<--- Score

8. What is your organizations system for selecting qualified vendors?
<--- Score

9. Identify an operational issue in your organization, for example, could a particular task be done more quickly or more efficiently by architecture competency?
<--- Score

10. Do you, as a leader, bounce back quickly from

setbacks?
<--- Score

11. How do you ensure that the architecture competency opportunity is realistic?
<--- Score

12. How do mission and objectives affect the architecture competency processes of your organization?
<--- Score

13. Do several people in different organizational units assist with the architecture competency process?
<--- Score

14. What qualifications are necessary?
<--- Score

15. How do you use architecture competency data and information to support organizational decision making and innovation?
<--- Score

16. Are you missing architecture competency opportunities?
<--- Score

17. What do you need to qualify?
<--- Score

18. How many input/output points does it require?
<--- Score

19. Has data output been validated?
<--- Score

20. What information qualified as important?
<--- Score

21. What were the crucial 'moments of truth' on the process map?
<--- Score

22. Which architecture competency data should be retained?
<--- Score

23. What resources go in to get the desired output?
<--- Score

24. Were any designed experiments used to generate additional insight into the data analysis?
<--- Score

25. What will drive architecture competency change?
<--- Score

26. What are the disruptive architecture competency technologies that enable your organization to radically change your business processes?
<--- Score

27. Where is architecture competency data gathered?
<--- Score

28. How will the architecture competency data be captured?
<--- Score

29. Has an output goal been set?
<--- Score

30. What architecture competency data do you gather or use now?
<--- Score

31. How is the way you as the leader think and process information affecting your organizational culture?
<--- Score

32. How much data can be collected in the given timeframe?
<--- Score

33. What is the complexity of the output produced?
<--- Score

34. What quality tools were used to get through the analyze phase?
<--- Score

35. Who is involved in the management review process?
<--- Score

36. What are your outputs?
<--- Score

37. What are the architecture competency business drivers?
<--- Score

38. Is pre-qualification of suppliers carried out?
<--- Score

39. An organizationally feasible system request is one that considers the mission, goals and objectives of the organization, key questions are: is the architecture competency solution request practical and will it solve a problem or take advantage of an opportunity to achieve company goals?

<--- Score

40. Who will gather what data?

<--- Score

41. What qualifies as competition?

<--- Score

42. How is the data gathered?

<--- Score

43. Are gaps between current performance and the goal performance identified?

<--- Score

44. How often will data be collected for measures?

<--- Score

45. Do quality systems drive continuous improvement?

<--- Score

46. What is the Value Stream Mapping?

<--- Score

47. How do you implement and manage your work processes to ensure that they meet design requirements?

<--- Score

48. How does the organization define, manage, and improve its architecture competency processes?
<--- Score

49. What architecture competency data should be collected?
<--- Score

50. What kind of crime could a potential new hire have committed that would not only not disqualify him/her from being hired by your organization, but would actually indicate that he/she might be a particularly good fit?
<--- Score

51. What methods do you use to gather architecture competency data?
<--- Score

52. What process should you select for improvement?
<--- Score

53. What is the output?
<--- Score

54. Do your employees have the opportunity to do what they do best everyday?
<--- Score

55. Should you invest in industry-recognized qualifications?
<--- Score

56. Think about some of the processes you undertake within your organization, which do you own?

<--- Score

57. What are the necessary qualifications?
<--- Score

58. What training and qualifications will you need?
<--- Score

59. Were there any improvement opportunities identified from the process analysis?
<--- Score

60. Are architecture competency changes recognized early enough to be approved through the regular process?
<--- Score

61. What architecture competency metrics are outputs of the process?
<--- Score

62. What internal processes need improvement?
<--- Score

63. What qualifications do architecture competency leaders need?
<--- Score

64. Who owns what data?
<--- Score

65. Are all staff in core architecture competency subjects Highly Qualified?
<--- Score

66. What other jobs or tasks affect the performance of

the steps in the architecture competency process?
<--- Score

67. What are the revised rough estimates of the financial savings/opportunity for architecture competency improvements?
<--- Score

68. How is the architecture competency Value Stream Mapping managed?
<--- Score

69. Was a cause-and-effect diagram used to explore the different types of causes (or sources of variation)?
<--- Score

70. Record-keeping requirements flow from the records needed as inputs, outputs, controls and for transformation of a architecture competency process, are the records needed as inputs to the architecture competency process available?
<--- Score

71. Do you understand your management processes today?
<--- Score

72. What qualifications are needed?
<--- Score

73. How has the architecture competency data been gathered?
<--- Score

74. What are your architecture competency processes?

<--- Score

75. What, related to, architecture competency processes does your organization outsource?
<--- Score

76. Where can you get qualified talent today?
<--- Score

77. What are your key performance measures or indicators and in-process measures for the control and improvement of your architecture competency processes?
<--- Score

78. Have the problem and goal statements been updated to reflect the additional knowledge gained from the analyze phase?
<--- Score

79. How is architecture competency data gathered?
<--- Score

80. What tools were used to generate the list of possible causes?
<--- Score

81. How are outputs preserved and protected?
<--- Score

82. What successful thing are you doing today that may be blinding you to new growth opportunities?
<--- Score

83. Do you have the authority to produce the output?
<--- Score

84. What are evaluation criteria for the output?
<--- Score

85. Is the final output clearly identified?
<--- Score

86. What systems/processes must you excel at?
<--- Score

87. What are the architecture competency design outputs?
<--- Score

88. What did the team gain from developing a sub-process map?
<--- Score

89. What other organizational variables, such as reward systems or communication systems, affect the performance of this architecture competency process?
<--- Score

90. How do you promote understanding that opportunity for improvement is not criticism of the status quo, or the people who created the status quo?
<--- Score

91. How do you identify specific architecture competency investment opportunities and emerging trends?
<--- Score

92. How do your work systems and key work processes relate to and capitalize on your core

competencies?

<--- Score

93. What were the financial benefits resulting from any 'ground fruit or low-hanging fruit' (quick fixes)?

<--- Score

94. What is the cost of poor quality as supported by the team's analysis?

<--- Score

95. Did any additional data need to be collected?

<--- Score

96. Is the performance gap determined?

<--- Score

97. Is the gap/opportunity displayed and communicated in financial terms?

<--- Score

98. What are the processes for audit reporting and management?

<--- Score

99. A compounding model resolution with available relevant data can often provide insight towards a solution methodology; which architecture competency models, tools and techniques are necessary?

<--- Score

100. Is there a strict change management process?

<--- Score

101. Who gets your output?

<--- Score

102. Do your leaders quickly bounce back from setbacks?
<--- Score

103. What types of data do your architecture competency indicators require?
<--- Score

104. Who is involved with workflow mapping?
<--- Score

105. What is the architecture competency Driver?
<--- Score

106. Were Pareto charts (or similar) used to portray the 'heavy hitters' (or key sources of variation)?
<--- Score

107. Is the required architecture competency data gathered?
<--- Score

108. What controls do you have in place to protect data?
<--- Score

109. Is data and process analysis, root cause analysis and quantifying the gap/opportunity in place?
<--- Score

110. Was a detailed process map created to amplify critical steps of the 'as is' stakeholder process?
<--- Score

111. What are the best opportunities for value improvement?
<--- Score

112. What does the data say about the performance of the stakeholder process?
<--- Score

113. Have any additional benefits been identified that will result from closing all or most of the gaps?
<--- Score

114. Where is the data coming from to measure compliance?
<--- Score

115. How do you define collaboration and team output?
<--- Score

116. How was the detailed process map generated, verified, and validated?
<--- Score

117. What conclusions were drawn from the team's data collection and analysis? How did the team reach these conclusions?
<--- Score

118. Is the architecture competency process severely broken such that a re-design is necessary?
<--- Score

119. What is the oversight process?
<--- Score

120. How can risk management be tied procedurally to process elements?
<--- Score

121. Are your outputs consistent?
<--- Score

122. How will the change process be managed?
<--- Score

123. How do you measure the operational performance of your key work systems and processes, including productivity, cycle time, and other appropriate measures of process effectiveness, efficiency, and innovation?
<--- Score

124. Who qualifies to gain access to data?
<--- Score

125. How is data used for program management and improvement?
<--- Score

126. What is your organizations process which leads to recognition of value generation?
<--- Score

127. Are all team members qualified for all tasks?
<--- Score

128. What process improvements will be needed?
<--- Score

129. What architecture competency data should be managed?

<--- Score

130. Do staff qualifications match your project?
<--- Score

131. Have you defined which data is gathered how?
<--- Score

132. Did any value-added analysis or 'lean thinking' take place to identify some of the gaps shown on the 'as is' process map?
<--- Score

133. What data is gathered?
<--- Score

134. What qualifications and skills do you need?
<--- Score

Add up total points for this section:
_ _ _ _ _ = Total points for this section

Divided by: _ _ _ _ _ _ (number of statements answered) = _ _ _ _ _ _
Average score for this section

Transfer your score to the architecture competency Index at the beginning of the Self-Assessment.

CRITERION #5: IMPROVE:

INTENT: Develop a practical solution. Innovate, establish and test the solution and to measure the results.

In my belief, the answer to this question is clearly defined:

5 Strongly Agree

4 Agree

3 Neutral

2 Disagree

1 Strongly Disagree

1. For decision problems, how do you develop a decision statement?
<--- Score

2. What practices helps your organization to develop its capacity to recognize patterns?
<--- Score

3. Can the solution be designed and implemented

within an acceptable time period?
<--- Score

4. What is architecture competency's impact on utilizing the best solution(s)?
<--- Score

5. What criteria will you use to assess your architecture competency risks?
<--- Score

6. To what extent does management recognize architecture competency as a tool to increase the results?
<--- Score

7. What does the 'should be' process map/design look like?
<--- Score

8. How can you improve performance?
<--- Score

9. What is the magnitude of the improvements?
<--- Score

10. Who are the architecture competency decision makers?
<--- Score

11. How do you go about comparing architecture competency approaches/solutions?
<--- Score

12. How will you measure the results?
<--- Score

13. How can the phases of architecture competency development be identified?
<--- Score

14. How is continuous improvement applied to risk management?
<--- Score

15. Were any criteria developed to assist the team in testing and evaluating potential solutions?
<--- Score

16. What to do with the results or outcomes of measurements?
<--- Score

17. Do vendor agreements bring new compliance risk ?
<--- Score

18. How is knowledge sharing about risk management improved?
<--- Score

19. Is the architecture competency documentation thorough?
<--- Score

20. Are the risks fully understood, reasonable and manageable?
<--- Score

21. Who controls the risk?
<--- Score

22. Explorations of the frontiers of architecture competency will help you build influence, improve architecture competency, optimize decision making, and sustain change, what is your approach?
<--- Score

23. What lessons, if any, from a pilot were incorporated into the design of the full-scale solution?
<--- Score

24. Who are the people involved in developing and implementing architecture competency?
<--- Score

25. Is risk periodically assessed?
<--- Score

26. How do you define the solutions' scope?
<--- Score

27. Who manages supplier risk management in your organization?
<--- Score

28. What are your current levels and trends in key measures or indicators of workforce and leader development?
<--- Score

29. Does a good decision guarantee a good outcome?
<--- Score

30. Which architecture competency solution is appropriate?
<--- Score

31. What strategies for architecture competency improvement are successful?
<--- Score

32. Is there a small-scale pilot for proposed improvement(s)? What conclusions were drawn from the outcomes of a pilot?
<--- Score

33. How do you improve productivity?
<--- Score

34. If you could go back in time five years, what decision would you make differently? What is your best guess as to what decision you're making today you might regret five years from now?
<--- Score

35. What needs improvement? Why?
<--- Score

36. Would you develop a architecture competency Communication Strategy?
<--- Score

37. Where do you need architecture competency improvement?
<--- Score

38. Are decisions made in a timely manner?
<--- Score

39. What area needs the greatest improvement?
<--- Score

40. What tools were used to tap into the creativity and encourage 'outside the box' thinking?
<--- Score

41. What is the implementation plan?
<--- Score

42. What are the expected architecture competency results?
<--- Score

43. Risk factors: what are the characteristics of architecture competency that make it risky?
<--- Score

44. Who will be responsible for documenting the architecture competency requirements in detail?
<--- Score

45. How will the group know that the solution worked?
<--- Score

46. Does the goal represent a desired result that can be measured?
<--- Score

47. What tools do you use once you have decided on a architecture competency strategy and more importantly how do you choose?
<--- Score

48. Can you identify any significant risks or exposures to architecture competency third- parties (vendors, service providers, alliance partners etc) that concern you?

<--- Score

49. Risk Identification: What are the possible
risk events your organization faces in relation to
architecture competency?
<--- Score

50. Are you assessing architecture competency and
risk?
<--- Score

**51. In the past few months, what is the smallest
change you have made that has had the biggest
positive result? What was it about that small
change that produced the large return?**
<--- Score

52. What should a proof of concept or pilot
accomplish?
<--- Score

53. What is architecture competency risk?
<--- Score

54. Are risk triggers captured?
<--- Score

55. What were the criteria for evaluating a architecture
competency pilot?
<--- Score

56. Who are the architecture competency decision-
makers?
<--- Score

57. Is the implementation plan designed?

<--- Score

58. Have you identified breakpoints and/or risk tolerances that will trigger broad consideration of a potential need for intervention or modification of strategy?
<--- Score

59. Is a contingency plan established?
<--- Score

60. Will the controls trigger any other risks?
<--- Score

61. Who controls key decisions that will be made?
<--- Score

62. What attendant changes will need to be made to ensure that the solution is successful?
<--- Score

63. How are policy decisions made and where?
<--- Score

64. Are events managed to resolution?
<--- Score

65. Who do you report architecture competency results to?
<--- Score

66. How will you know that a change is an improvement?
<--- Score

67. Is supporting architecture competency

documentation required?
<--- Score

68. At what point will vulnerability assessments be performed once architecture competency is put into production (e.g., ongoing Risk Management after implementation)?
<--- Score

69. Who manages architecture competency risk?
<--- Score

70. How do you mitigate architecture competency risk?
<--- Score

71. When you map the key players in your own work and the types/domains of relationships with them, which relationships do you find easy and which challenging, and why?
<--- Score

72. Are risk management tasks balanced centrally and locally?
<--- Score

73. How do you manage architecture competency risk?
<--- Score

74. Do you need to do a usability evaluation?
<--- Score

75. What communications are necessary to support the implementation of the solution?
<--- Score

76. What went well, what should change, what can improve?
<--- Score

77. Is the optimal solution selected based on testing and analysis?
<--- Score

78. How do you measure risk?
<--- Score

79. How scalable is your architecture competency solution?
<--- Score

80. Is there a high likelihood that any recommendations will achieve their intended results?
<--- Score

81. How do you keep improving architecture competency?
<--- Score

82. Was a architecture competency charter developed?
<--- Score

83. How significant is the improvement in the eyes of the end user?
<--- Score

84. Why improve in the first place?
<--- Score

85. Is architecture competency documentation maintained?
<--- Score

86. How will you know when its improved?
<--- Score

87. Is the solution technically practical?
<--- Score

88. What is the architecture competency's sustainability risk?
<--- Score

89. Have you achieved architecture competency improvements?
<--- Score

90. What tools were most useful during the improve phase?
<--- Score

91. How do you deal with architecture competency risk?
<--- Score

92. How can skill-level changes improve architecture competency?
<--- Score

93. How do the architecture competency results compare with the performance of your competitors and other organizations with similar offerings?
<--- Score

94. How do you measure progress and evaluate

training effectiveness?
<--- Score

95. What resources are required for the improvement efforts?
<--- Score

96. How risky is your organization?
<--- Score

97. Is there a cost/benefit analysis of optimal solution(s)?
<--- Score

98. Do you have the optimal project management team structure?
<--- Score

99. For estimation problems, how do you develop an estimation statement?
<--- Score

100. How do you link measurement and risk?
<--- Score

101. What architecture competency improvements can be made?
<--- Score

102. What error proofing will be done to address some of the discrepancies observed in the 'as is' process?
<--- Score

103. How do you improve your likelihood of success ?
<--- Score

104. What improvements have been achieved?
<--- Score

105. Is a solution implementation plan established, including schedule/work breakdown structure, resources, risk management plan, cost/budget, and control plan?
<--- Score

106. What are the architecture competency security risks?
<--- Score

107. What were the underlying assumptions on the cost-benefit analysis?
<--- Score

108. Who are the key stakeholders for the architecture competency evaluation?
<--- Score

109. architecture competency risk decisions: whose call Is It?
<--- Score

110. What are the implications of the one critical architecture competency decision 10 minutes, 10 months, and 10 years from now?
<--- Score

111. How can you better manage risk?
<--- Score

112. Is any architecture competency documentation required?
<--- Score

113. What actually has to improve and by how much?

<--- Score

114. What do you want to improve?

<--- Score

115. Who should make the architecture competency decisions?

<--- Score

116. Where do the architecture competency decisions reside?

<--- Score

117. Do you combine technical expertise with business knowledge and architecture competency Key topics include lifecycles, development approaches, requirements and how to make a business case?

<--- Score

118. Who makes the architecture competency decisions in your organization?

<--- Score

119. How will you recognize and celebrate results?

<--- Score

120. Is the measure of success for architecture competency understandable to a variety of people?

<--- Score

121. What is the team's contingency plan for potential

problems occurring in implementation?
<--- Score

122. How do you manage and improve your architecture competency work systems to deliver customer value and achieve organizational success and sustainability?
<--- Score

123. What are the concrete architecture competency results?
<--- Score

124. How do you measure improved architecture competency service perception, and satisfaction?
<--- Score

125. Is the scope clearly documented?
<--- Score

126. What current systems have to be understood and/or changed?
<--- Score

127. How are architecture competency risks managed?
<--- Score

128. Is pilot data collected and analyzed?
<--- Score

129. How can you improve architecture competency?
<--- Score

130. What are the affordable architecture

competency risks?
<--- Score

131. Are the most efficient solutions problem-specific?
<--- Score

132. What tools were used to evaluate the potential solutions?
<--- Score

133. What can you do to improve?
<--- Score

134. Was a pilot designed for the proposed solution(s)?
<--- Score

135. Risk events: what are the things that could go wrong?
<--- Score

136. Is the architecture competency risk managed?
<--- Score

137. How will the team or the process owner(s) monitor the implementation plan to see that it is working as intended?
<--- Score

138. Is the architecture competency solution sustainable?
<--- Score

139. Which of the recognised risks out of all risks can be most likely transferred?
<--- Score

140. Are procedures documented for managing architecture competency risks?
<--- Score

141. Do those selected for the architecture competency team have a good general understanding of what architecture competency is all about?
<--- Score

142. How do you decide how much to remunerate an employee?
<--- Score

Add up total points for this section:
_ _ _ _ _ = Total points for this section

Divided by: _ _ _ _ _ _ (number of statements answered) = _ _ _ _ _ _
Average score for this section

Transfer your score to the architecture competency Index at the beginning of the Self-Assessment.

CRITERION #6: CONTROL:

INTENT: Implement the practical solution. Maintain the performance and correct possible complications.

In my belief, the answer to this question is clearly defined:

5 Strongly Agree

4 Agree

3 Neutral

2 Disagree

1 Strongly Disagree

1. How will you measure your QA plan's effectiveness?
<--- Score

2. Are pertinent alerts monitored, analyzed and distributed to appropriate personnel?
<--- Score

3. Against what alternative is success being measured?

<--- Score

4. What quality tools were useful in the control phase?
<--- Score

5. How will new or emerging customer needs/
requirements be checked/communicated to orient
the process toward meeting the new specifications
and continually reducing variation?
<--- Score

6. Where do ideas that reach policy makers and
planners as proposals for architecture competency
strengthening and reform actually originate?
<--- Score

7. How will the process owner and team be able to
hold the gains?
<--- Score

8. How likely is the current architecture competency
plan to come in on schedule or on budget?
<--- Score

9. Are the planned controls working?
<--- Score

10. Is knowledge gained on process shared and
institutionalized?
<--- Score

11. How will report readings be checked to effectively
monitor performance?
<--- Score

12. What is the control/monitoring plan?

<--- Score

13. How widespread is its use?
<--- Score

14. How might the group capture best practices and lessons learned so as to leverage improvements?
<--- Score

15. What other systems, operations, processes, and infrastructures (hiring practices, staffing, training, incentives/rewards, metrics/dashboards/scorecards, etc.) need updates, additions, changes, or deletions in order to facilitate knowledge transfer and improvements?
<--- Score

16. What are customers monitoring?
<--- Score

17. How is architecture competency project cost planned, managed, monitored?
<--- Score

18. What is your plan to assess your security risks?
<--- Score

19. Is reporting being used or needed?
<--- Score

20. Is a response plan in place for when the input, process, or output measures indicate an 'out-of-control' condition?
<--- Score

21. How do you select, collect, align, and integrate

architecture competency data and information for tracking daily operations and overall organizational performance, including progress relative to strategic objectives and action plans?
<--- Score

22. Has the improved process and its steps been standardized?
<--- Score

23. Do the viable solutions scale to future needs?
<--- Score

24. Can you adapt and adjust to changing architecture competency situations?
<--- Score

25. What is the standard for acceptable architecture competency performance?
<--- Score

26. What architecture competency standards are applicable?
<--- Score

27. What are the performance and scale of the architecture competency tools?
<--- Score

28. How will input, process, and output variables be checked to detect for sub-optimal conditions?
<--- Score

29. Is the architecture competency test/monitoring cost justified?
<--- Score

30. How do you spread information?
<--- Score

31. What is the recommended frequency of auditing?
<--- Score

32. Act/Adjust: What Do you Need to Do Differently?
<--- Score

33. Will existing staff require re-training, for example, to learn new business processes?
<--- Score

34. Are the architecture competency standards challenging?
<--- Score

35. How do your controls stack up?
<--- Score

36. Is a response plan established and deployed?
<--- Score

37. How will architecture competency decisions be made and monitored?
<--- Score

38. How is change control managed?
<--- Score

39. Who is going to spread your message?
<--- Score

40. Is there a standardized process?
<--- Score

41. What is the best design framework for architecture competency organization now that, in a post industrial-age if the top-down, command and control model is no longer relevant?
<--- Score

42. What do you measure to verify effectiveness gains?
<--- Score

43. What are you attempting to measure/monitor?
<--- Score

44. How do controls support value?
<--- Score

45. What do you stand for--and what are you against?
<--- Score

46. Is there documentation that will support the successful operation of the improvement?
<--- Score

47. Is there a control plan in place for sustaining improvements (short and long-term)?
<--- Score

48. How do you establish and deploy modified action plans if circumstances require a shift in plans and rapid execution of new plans?
<--- Score

49. What key inputs and outputs are being measured on an ongoing basis?

<--- Score

50. Is there a recommended audit plan for routine surveillance inspections of architecture competency's gains?
<--- Score

51. Are documented procedures clear and easy to follow for the operators?
<--- Score

52. Is there an action plan in case of emergencies?
<--- Score

53. Is there a transfer of ownership and knowledge to process owner and process team tasked with the responsibilities.
<--- Score

54. Are controls in place and consistently applied?
<--- Score

55. Is there a architecture competency Communication plan covering who needs to get what information when?
<--- Score

56. Are new process steps, standards, and documentation ingrained into normal operations?
<--- Score

57. Does a troubleshooting guide exist or is it needed?
<--- Score

58. Are the planned controls in place?
<--- Score

59. Will your goals reflect your program budget?
<--- Score

60. What adjustments to the strategies are needed?
<--- Score

61. Who controls critical resources?
<--- Score

62. What are the critical parameters to watch?
<--- Score

63. What can you control?
<--- Score

64. Who sets the architecture competency standards?
<--- Score

65. Is new knowledge gained imbedded in the response plan?
<--- Score

66. Who will be in control?
<--- Score

67. How will the process owner verify improvement in present and future sigma levels, process capabilities?
<--- Score

68. How do you encourage people to take control and responsibility?
<--- Score

69. Are suggested corrective/restorative actions

indicated on the response plan for known causes to problems that might surface?
<--- Score

70. In the case of a architecture competency project, the criteria for the audit derive from implementation objectives, an audit of a architecture competency project involves assessing whether the recommendations outlined for implementation have been met, can you track that any architecture competency project is implemented as planned, and is it working?
<--- Score

71. Will any special training be provided for results interpretation?
<--- Score

72. Who is the architecture competency process owner?
<--- Score

73. How do senior leaders actions reflect a commitment to the organizations architecture competency values?
<--- Score

74. You may have created your quality measures at a time when you lacked resources, technology wasn't up to the required standard, or low service levels were the industry norm. Have those circumstances changed?
<--- Score

75. Do you monitor the effectiveness of your architecture competency activities?

<--- Score

76. Implementation Planning: is a pilot needed to test the changes before a full roll out occurs?
<--- Score

77. Does the architecture competency performance meet the customer's requirements?
<--- Score

78. How do you plan for the cost of succession?
<--- Score

79. How can you best use all of your knowledge repositories to enhance learning and sharing?
<--- Score

80. Have new or revised work instructions resulted?
<--- Score

81. Are there documented procedures?
<--- Score

82. Are operating procedures consistent?
<--- Score

83. How will the day-to-day responsibilities for monitoring and continual improvement be transferred from the improvement team to the process owner?
<--- Score

84. What should you measure to verify efficiency gains?
<--- Score

85. What should the next improvement project be that is related to architecture competency?
<--- Score

86. Does the response plan contain a definite closed loop continual improvement scheme (e.g., plan-do-check-act)?
<--- Score

87. Are you measuring, monitoring and predicting architecture competency activities to optimize operations and profitability, and enhancing outcomes?
<--- Score

88. Does architecture competency appropriately measure and monitor risk?
<--- Score

89. What are the known security controls?
<--- Score

90. How do you monitor usage and cost?
<--- Score

91. Do the architecture competency decisions you make today help people and the planet tomorrow?
<--- Score

92. What is your theory of human motivation, and how does your compensation plan fit with that view?
<--- Score

93. What are the key elements of your architecture competency performance improvement system, including your evaluation, organizational

learning, and innovation processes?
<--- Score

94. Do you monitor the architecture competency decisions made and fine tune them as they evolve?
<--- Score

95. Does job training on the documented procedures need to be part of the process team's education and training?
<--- Score

96. What other areas of the group might benefit from the architecture competency team's improvements, knowledge, and learning?
<--- Score

97. Who has control over resources?
<--- Score

98. Can support from partners be adjusted?
<--- Score

99. How do you plan on providing proper recognition and disclosure of supporting companies?
<--- Score

100. Is there a documented and implemented monitoring plan?
<--- Score

Add up total points for this section:
_ _ _ _ _ = Total points for this section

Divided by: _ _ _ _ _ _ (number of statements answered) = _ _ _ _ _ _

Average score for this section

Transfer your score to the architecture
competency Index at the beginning of
the Self-Assessment.

CRITERION #7: SUSTAIN:

INTENT: Retain the benefits.

In my belief, the answer to this question is clearly defined:

5 Strongly Agree

4 Agree

3 Neutral

2 Disagree

1 Strongly Disagree

1. Whom among your colleagues do you trust, and for what?
<--- Score

2. Who are your customers?
<--- Score

3. Operational - will it work?
<--- Score

4. How do you maintain architecture competency's

Integrity?
<--- Score

5. Are you / should you be revolutionary or evolutionary?
<--- Score

6. Is a architecture competency breakthrough on the horizon?
<--- Score

7. At what moment would you think; Will I get fired?
<--- Score

8. Can you do all this work?
<--- Score

9. How do you accomplish your long range architecture competency goals?
<--- Score

10. What could happen if you do not do it?
<--- Score

11. Who is responsible for architecture competency?
<--- Score

12. Whose voice (department, ethnic group, women, older workers, etc) might you have missed hearing from in your company, and how might you amplify this voice to create positive momentum for your business?
<--- Score

13. What is the craziest thing you can do?
<--- Score

14. Who will be responsible for deciding whether architecture competency goes ahead or not after the initial investigations?
<--- Score

15. What are the essentials of internal architecture competency management?
<--- Score

16. How can you become more high-tech but still be high touch?
<--- Score

17. What you are going to do to affect the numbers?
<--- Score

18. In a project to restructure architecture competency outcomes, which stakeholders would you involve?
<--- Score

19. What information is critical to your organization that your executives are ignoring?
<--- Score

20. What are you trying to prove to yourself, and how might it be hijacking your life and business success?
<--- Score

21. What are the usability implications of architecture competency actions?
<--- Score

22. What stupid rule would you most like to kill?

<--- Score

23. Who is responsible for ensuring appropriate resources (time, people and money) are allocated to architecture competency?
<--- Score

24. Which functions and people interact with the supplier and or customer?
<--- Score

25. Is the impact that architecture competency has shown?
<--- Score

26. How do you keep the momentum going?
<--- Score

27. How do you determine the key elements that affect architecture competency workforce satisfaction, how are these elements determined for different workforce groups and segments?
<--- Score

28. If you do not follow, then how to lead?
<--- Score

29. Why will customers want to buy your organizations products/services?
<--- Score

30. How do you listen to customers to obtain actionable information?
<--- Score

31. What happens when a new employee joins the

organization?

<--- Score

32. What architecture competency skills are most important?

<--- Score

33. What are current architecture competency paradigms?

<--- Score

34. What are specific architecture competency rules to follow?

<--- Score

35. Which individuals, teams or departments will be involved in architecture competency?

<--- Score

36. How do you engage the workforce, in addition to satisfying them?

<--- Score

37. Are your responses positive or negative?

<--- Score

38. How can you negotiate architecture competency successfully with a stubborn boss, an irate client, or a deceitful coworker?

<--- Score

39. How do you ensure that implementations of architecture competency products are done in a way that ensures safety?

<--- Score

40. How important is architecture competency to the user organizations mission?
<--- Score

41. Are the assumptions believable and achievable?
<--- Score

42. How do you deal with architecture competency changes?
<--- Score

43. What potential megatrends could make your business model obsolete?
<--- Score

44. What is your competitive advantage?
<--- Score

45. What happens if you do not have enough funding?
<--- Score

46. How do you create buy-in?
<--- Score

47. What are the barriers to increased architecture competency production?
<--- Score

48. In retrospect, of the projects that you pulled the plug on, what percent do you wish had been allowed to keep going, and what percent do you wish had ended earlier?
<--- Score

49. Are you paying enough attention to the partners

your company depends on to succeed?
<--- Score

50. Are you making progress, and are you making progress as architecture competency leaders?
<--- Score

51. Which models, tools and techniques are necessary?
<--- Score

52. Has implementation been effective in reaching specified objectives so far?
<--- Score

53. If you had to rebuild your organization without any traditional competitive advantages (i.e., no killer technology, promising research, innovative product/ service delivery model, etcetera), how would your people have to approach their work and collaborate together in order to create the necessary conditions for success?
<--- Score

54. How do you provide a safe environment -physically and emotionally?
<--- Score

55. Are you relevant? Will you be relevant five years from now? Ten?
<--- Score

56. Have new benefits been realized?
<--- Score

57. How do you lead with architecture competency in

mind?

<--- Score

58. Why do and why don't your customers like your organization?

<--- Score

59. What new services of functionality will be implemented next with architecture competency ?

<--- Score

60. What does your signature ensure?

<--- Score

61. How do you go about securing architecture competency?

<--- Score

62. Who else should you help?

<--- Score

63. Will there be any necessary staff changes (redundancies or new hires)?

<--- Score

64. If you find that you havent accomplished one of the goals for one of the steps of the architecture competency strategy, what will you do to fix it?

<--- Score

65. Were lessons learned captured and communicated?

<--- Score

66. How do you govern and fulfill your societal responsibilities?

<--- Score

67. Who do we want your customers to become?
<--- Score

68. Why should you adopt a architecture competency framework?
<--- Score

69. If you were responsible for initiating and implementing major changes in your organization, what steps might you take to ensure acceptance of those changes?
<--- Score

70. What is the overall talent health of your organization as a whole at senior levels, and for each organization reporting to a member of the Senior Leadership Team?
<--- Score

71. What are the key enablers to make this architecture competency move?
<--- Score

72. What will be the consequences to the stakeholder (financial, reputation etc) if architecture competency does not go ahead or fails to deliver the objectives?
<--- Score

73. What are the short and long-term architecture competency goals?
<--- Score

74. How can you incorporate support to ensure safe and effective use of architecture competency into the

services that you provide?
<--- Score

75. Is it economical; do you have the time and money?
<--- Score

76. What one word do you want to own in the minds of your customers, employees, and partners?
<--- Score

77. How do you track customer value, profitability or financial return, organizational success, and sustainability?
<--- Score

78. How will you insure seamless interoperability of architecture competency moving forward?
<--- Score

79. What are the long-term architecture competency goals?
<--- Score

80. What do we do when new problems arise?
<--- Score

81. How long will it take to change?
<--- Score

82. How do you manage architecture competency Knowledge Management (KM)?
<--- Score

83. Can the schedule be done in the given time?
<--- Score

84. What may be the consequences for the performance of an organization if all stakeholders are not consulted regarding architecture competency?
<--- Score

85. What is your formula for success in architecture competency ?
<--- Score

86. What is the kind of project structure that would be appropriate for your architecture competency project, should it be formal and complex, or can it be less formal and relatively simple?
<--- Score

87. What is effective architecture competency?
<--- Score

88. What are your most important goals for the strategic architecture competency objectives?
<--- Score

89. How do you proactively clarify deliverables and architecture competency quality expectations?
<--- Score

90. What are the success criteria that will indicate that architecture competency objectives have been met and the benefits delivered?
<--- Score

91. What management system can you use to leverage the architecture competency experience, ideas, and concerns of the people closest to the work to be done?
<--- Score

92. What is the source of the strategies for architecture competency strengthening and reform?
<--- Score

93. What architecture competency modifications can you make work for you?
<--- Score

94. What are your personal philosophies regarding architecture competency and how do they influence your work?
<--- Score

95. Which architecture competency goals are the most important?
<--- Score

96. Who do you think the world wants your organization to be?
<--- Score

97. Have benefits been optimized with all key stakeholders?
<--- Score

98. Where can you break convention?
<--- Score

99. Is your basic point _____ or _____?
<--- Score

100. What are the gaps in your knowledge and experience?
<--- Score

101. What are strategies for increasing support and reducing opposition?
<--- Score

102. Do you know who is a friend or a foe?
<--- Score

103. Do architecture competency rules make a reasonable demand on a users capabilities?
<--- Score

104. Do you see more potential in people than they do in themselves?
<--- Score

105. How do you set architecture competency stretch targets and how do you get people to not only participate in setting these stretch targets but also that they strive to achieve these?
<--- Score

106. Who is the main stakeholder, with ultimate responsibility for driving architecture competency forward?
<--- Score

107. Are you maintaining a past–present– future perspective throughout the architecture competency discussion?
<--- Score

108. What is something you believe that nearly no one agrees with you on?
<--- Score

109. Is maximizing architecture competency

protection the same as minimizing architecture competency loss?
<--- Score

110. Who are four people whose careers you have enhanced?
<--- Score

111. How do you foster innovation?
<--- Score

112. What is your architecture competency strategy?
<--- Score

113. What threat is architecture competency addressing?
<--- Score

114. What was the last experiment you ran?
<--- Score

115. What did you miss in the interview for the worst hire you ever made?
<--- Score

116. What have been your experiences in defining long range architecture competency goals?
<--- Score

117. Do you have enough freaky customers in your portfolio pushing you to the limit day in and day out?
<--- Score

118. Is architecture competency dependent on the successful delivery of a current project?
<--- Score

119. How are you doing compared to your industry?
<--- Score

120. How do you make it meaningful in connecting architecture competency with what users do day-to-day?
<--- Score

121. What have you done to protect your business from competitive encroachment?
<--- Score

122. Why not do architecture competency?
<--- Score

123. Is a architecture competency team work effort in place?
<--- Score

124. How will you motivate the stakeholders with the least vested interest?
<--- Score

125. Can you maintain your growth without detracting from the factors that have contributed to your success?
<--- Score

126. Who uses your product in ways you never expected?
<--- Score

127. How do customers see your organization?
<--- Score

128. Are you changing as fast as the world around you?
<--- Score

129. Do you feel that more should be done in the architecture competency area?
<--- Score

130. Why is architecture competency important for you now?
<--- Score

131. What unique value proposition (UVP) do you offer?
<--- Score

132. How do you keep records, of what?
<--- Score

133. How much contingency will be available in the budget?
<--- Score

134. What happens at your organization when people fail?
<--- Score

135. Why is it important to have senior management support for a architecture competency project?
<--- Score

136. What is a feasible sequencing of reform initiatives over time?
<--- Score

137. How can you become the company that would

put you out of business?
<--- Score

138. Will it be accepted by users?
<--- Score

139. Who, on the executive team or the board, has spoken to a customer recently?
<--- Score

140. What role does communication play in the success or failure of a architecture competency project?
<--- Score

141. What are the business goals architecture competency is aiming to achieve?
<--- Score

142. What are the top 3 things at the forefront of your architecture competency agendas for the next 3 years?
<--- Score

143. Are all key stakeholders present at all Structured Walkthroughs?
<--- Score

144. Ask yourself: how would you do this work if you only had one staff member to do it?
<--- Score

145. What is your question? Why?
<--- Score

146. How do you cross-sell and up-sell your

architecture competency success?
<--- Score

147. If you got fired and a new hire took your place, what would she do different?
<--- Score

148. Are new benefits received and understood?
<--- Score

149. What is the purpose of architecture competency in relation to the mission?
<--- Score

150. Can you break it down?
<--- Score

151. How do you transition from the baseline to the target?
<--- Score

152. What goals did you miss?
<--- Score

153. What is the funding source for this project?
<--- Score

154. Are you using a design thinking approach and integrating Innovation, architecture competency Experience, and Brand Value?
<--- Score

155. Did your employees make progress today?
<--- Score

156. Who are the key stakeholders?

<--- Score

157. Is architecture competency realistic, or are you setting yourself up for failure?
<--- Score

158. Do you have an implicit bias for capital investments over people investments?
<--- Score

159. What relationships among architecture competency trends do you perceive?
<--- Score

160. Is the architecture competency organization completing tasks effectively and efficiently?
<--- Score

161. Does a architecture competency quantification method exist?
<--- Score

162. Are you satisfied with your current role? If not, what is missing from it?
<--- Score

163. If there were zero limitations, what would you do differently?
<--- Score

164. Who will determine interim and final deadlines?
<--- Score

165. What are the rules and assumptions your industry operates under? What if the opposite were true?
<--- Score

166. What is the estimated value of the project?
<--- Score

167. Would you rather sell to knowledgeable and informed customers or to uninformed customers?
<--- Score

168. Who is on the team?
<--- Score

169. Why should people listen to you?
<--- Score

170. Do you have past architecture competency successes?
<--- Score

171. Who will manage the integration of tools?
<--- Score

172. How likely is it that a customer would recommend your company to a friend or colleague?
<--- Score

173. What trophy do you want on your mantle?
<--- Score

174. If your company went out of business tomorrow, would anyone who doesn't get a paycheck here care?
<--- Score

175. Instead of going to current contacts for new ideas, what if you reconnected with dormant contacts--the people you used to know? If you were going reactivate a dormant tie, who would it

be?
<--- Score

176. Do you have the right capabilities and capacities?
<--- Score

177. When information truly is ubiquitous, when reach and connectivity are completely global, when computing resources are infinite, and when a whole new set of impossibilities are not only possible, but happening, what will that do to your business?
<--- Score

178. Think of your architecture competency project, what are the main functions?
<--- Score

179. Is your strategy driving your strategy? Or is the way in which you allocate resources driving your strategy?
<--- Score

180. How does architecture competency integrate with other stakeholder initiatives?
<--- Score

181. What are the potential basics of architecture competency fraud?
<--- Score

182. How do you assess the architecture competency pitfalls that are inherent in implementing it?
<--- Score

183. What should you stop doing?

<--- Score

184. Are there any activities that you can take off your to do list?
<--- Score

185. What trouble can you get into?
<--- Score

186. What business benefits will architecture competency goals deliver if achieved?
<--- Score

187. What projects are going on in the organization today, and what resources are those projects using from the resource pools?
<--- Score

188. Do you have the right people on the bus?
<--- Score

189. Do you think architecture competency accomplishes the goals you expect it to accomplish?
<--- Score

190. How do senior leaders deploy your organizations vision and values through your leadership system, to the workforce, to key suppliers and partners, and to customers and other stakeholders, as appropriate?
<--- Score

191. How will you ensure you get what you expected?
<--- Score

192. Do you know what you are doing? And who do

you call if you don't?
<--- Score

193. What is the big architecture competency idea?
<--- Score

194. Who is responsible for errors?
<--- Score

195. What are internal and external architecture competency relations?
<--- Score

196. Who do you want your customers to become?
<--- Score

197. What must you excel at?
<--- Score

198. If no one would ever find out about your accomplishments, how would you lead differently?
<--- Score

199. How do you stay inspired?
<--- Score

200. In the past year, what have you done (or could you have done) to increase the accurate perception of your company/brand as ethical and honest?
<--- Score

201. If you had to leave your organization for a year and the only communication you could have with employees/colleagues was a single paragraph, what would you write?

<--- Score

202. How do you know if you are successful?
<--- Score

203. What is it like to work for you?
<--- Score

204. What are you challenging?
<--- Score

205. Who have you, as a company, historically been when you've been at your best?
<--- Score

206. Is there any reason to believe the opposite of my current belief?
<--- Score

207. What would have to be true for the option on the table to be the best possible choice?
<--- Score

208. Is there any existing architecture competency governance structure?
<--- Score

209. What knowledge, skills and characteristics mark a good architecture competency project manager?
<--- Score

210. What is the range of capabilities?
<--- Score

Add up total points for this section:
_ _ _ _ _ = Total points for this section

Divided by: _____ (number of
statements answered) = _____
Average score for this section

Transfer your score to the architecture
competency Index at the beginning of
the Self-Assessment.

Architecture Competency and Managing Projects, Criteria for Project Managers:

1.0 Initiating Process Group: Architecture Competency

1. What were things that you did well, and could improve, and how?

2. What areas does the group agree are the biggest success on the Architecture Competency project?

3. Do you understand all business (operational), technical, resource and vendor risks associated with the Architecture Competency project?

4. What input will you be required to provide the Architecture Competency project team?

5. What will you do?

6. When must it be done?

7. What business situation is being addressed?

8. What are the short and long term implications?

9. Are identified risks being monitored properly, are new risks arising during the Architecture Competency project or are foreseen risks occurring?

10. In which Architecture Competency project management process group is the detailed Architecture Competency project budget created?

11. What communication items need improvement?

12. Who supports, improves, and oversees

standardized processes related to the Architecture Competency projects program?

13. Who is behind the Architecture Competency project?

14. When will the Architecture Competency project be done?

15. Were escalated issues resolved promptly?

16. Were resources available as planned?

17. Measurable - are the targets measurable?

18. What are the tools and techniques to be used in each phase?

19. Are stakeholders properly informed about the status of the Architecture Competency project?

20. How will it affect me?

1.1 Project Charter: Architecture Competency

21. Why is a Architecture Competency project Charter used?

22. Why do you manage integration?

23. Review the general mission What system will be affected by the improvement efforts?

24. Who ise input and support will this Architecture Competency project require?

25. Must Have?

26. What are the known stakeholder requirements?

27. What changes can you make to improve?

28. When?

29. Success determination factors: how will the success of the Architecture Competency project be determined from the customers perspective?

30. What is the justification?

31. Does the Architecture Competency project need to consider any special capacity or capability issues?

32. Who is the sponsor?

33. What is the business need?

34. What are the assigned resources?

35. Avoid costs, improve service, and/ or comply with a mandate?

36. Dependent Architecture Competency projects: what Architecture Competency projects must be underway or completed before this Architecture Competency project can be successful?

37. Are you building in-house ?

38. Why have you chosen the aim you have set forth?

39. What are some examples of a business case?

1.2 Stakeholder Register: Architecture Competency

40. Who is managing stakeholder engagement?

41. What is the power of the stakeholder?

42. How much influence do they have on the Architecture Competency project?

43. How will reports be created?

44. What are the major Architecture Competency project milestones requiring communications or providing communications opportunities?

45. Is your organization ready for change?

46. How big is the gap?

47. Who are the stakeholders?

48. Who wants to talk about Security?

49. How should employers make voices heard?

50. What opportunities exist to provide communications?

51. What & Why?

1.3 Stakeholder Analysis Matrix: Architecture Competency

52. Who has been involved in the area (thematic or geographic) in the past?

53. Accreditations, etc?

54. What do you Evaluate?

55. Vital contracts and partners?

56. What is the stakeholders power and status in relation to the Architecture Competency project?

57. Inoculations or payment to receive them?

58. What actions can be taken to reduce or mitigate risk?

59. How will the Architecture Competency project benefit them?

60. Who can contribute financial or technical resources towards the work?

61. Who has not been involved up to now and should have been?

62. Economy - home, abroad?

63. Vulnerable groups; who are the vulnerable groups that might be affected by the Architecture

Competency project?

64. Who will be responsible for managing the outcome?

65. How do they affect the Architecture Competency project and its outcomes?

66. Benefit to whom?

67. Morale, commitment, leadership?

68. Competitors vulnerabilities?

69. Which conditions out of the control of the management are crucial for the achievement of the immediate objective?

70. Financial reserves, likely returns?

71. How to involve media?

2.0 Planning Process Group: Architecture Competency

72. To what extent are the visions and actions of the partners consistent or divergent with regard to the program?

73. The Architecture Competency project charter is created in which Architecture Competency project management process group?

74. Do the partners have sufficient financial capacity to keep up the benefits produced by the programme?

75. In which Architecture Competency project management process group is the detailed Architecture Competency project budget created?

76. How will it affect you?

77. Does it make any difference if you are successful?

78. Mitigate. what will you do to minimize the impact should a risk event occur?

79. On which process should team members spend the most time?

80. Will you be replaced?

81. To what extent have the target population and participants made the activities own, taking an active role in it?

82. Why is it important to determine activity sequencing on Architecture Competency projects?

83. How will users learn how to use the deliverables?

84. What are the different approaches to building the WBS?

85. If you are late, will anybody notice?

86. What is the NEXT thing to do?

87. How will you do it?

88. You did your readings, yes?

89. First of all, should any action be taken?

90. When will the Architecture Competency project be done?

91. To what extent is the program helping to influence your organizations policy framework?

2.1 Project Management Plan: Architecture Competency

92. What are the assumptions?

93. What did not work so well?

94. What went wrong?

95. What is risk management?

96. What would you do differently what did not work?

97. Are calculations and results of analyzes essentially correct?

98. If the Architecture Competency project is complex or scope is specialized, do you have appropriate and/or qualified staff available to perform the tasks?

99. Is the engineering content at a feasibility level-of-detail, and is it sufficiently complete, to provide an adequate basis for the baseline cost estimate?

100. Why Change?

101. Are the proposed Architecture Competency project purposes different than a previously authorized Architecture Competency project?

102. Development trends and opportunities. What if the positive direction and vision of your organization causes expected trends to change?

103. What is Architecture Competency project scope management?

104. Are there any client staffing expectations?

105. How do you organize the costs in the Architecture Competency project management plan?

106. Are there any windfall benefits that would accrue to the Architecture Competency project sponsor or other parties?

107. Who is the Architecture Competency project Manager?

108. What worked well?

109. Are the existing and future without-plan conditions reasonable and appropriate?

2.2 Scope Management Plan: Architecture Competency

110. How difficult will it be to do specific activities on this Architecture Competency project?

111. Is an industry recognized mechanized support tool(s) being used for Architecture Competency project scheduling & tracking?

112. Are risk triggers captured?

113. Are measurements and feedback mechanisms incorporated in tracking work effort & refining work estimating techniques?

114. Does a documented Architecture Competency project organizational policy & plan (i.e. governance model) exist?

115. Are enough systems & user personnel assigned to the Architecture Competency project?

116. What weaknesses do you have?

117. Has a quality assurance plan been developed for the Architecture Competency project?

118. Are internal Architecture Competency project status meetings held at reasonable intervals?

119. Cost / benefit analysis?

120. What are the risks that could significantly affect the budget of the Architecture Competency project?

121. Are alternatives safe, functional, constructible, economical, reasonable and sustainable?

122. Has the Architecture Competency project scope been baselined?

123. Are any non-compliance issues that exist due to organizations practices?

124. What problem is being solved by delivering this Architecture Competency project?

125. Are post milestone Architecture Competency project reviews (PMPR) conducted with your organization at least once a year?

126. Product – what are you trying to accomplish and how will you know when you are finished?

127. Is it standard practice to formally commit stakeholders to the Architecture Competency project via agreements?

128. Have the scope, objectives, costs, benefits and impacts been communicated to all involved and/or impacted stakeholders and work groups?

129. Are schedule deliverables actually delivered?

2.3 Requirements Management Plan: Architecture Competency

130. Who will do the reporting and to whom will reports be delivered?

131. What information regarding the Architecture Competency project requirements will be reported?

132. Will the product release be stable and mature enough to be deployed in the user community?

133. How will you develop the schedule of requirements activities?

134. How will unresolved questions be handled once approval has been obtained?

135. How often will the reporting occur?

136. Define the help desk model. who will take full responsibility?

137. Is requirements work dependent on any other specific Architecture Competency project or non-Architecture Competency project activities (e.g. funding, approvals, procurement)?

138. Did you get proper approvals?

139. What is the earliest finish date for this Architecture Competency project if it is scheduled to start on ...?

140. Do you have price sheets and a methodology for determining the total proposal cost?

141. Did you distinguish the scope of work the contractor(s) will be required to do?

142. What performance metrics will be used?

143. Is stakeholder risk tolerance an important factor for the requirements process in this Architecture Competency project?

144. Are actual resources expenditures versus planned expenditures acceptable?

145. How detailed should the Architecture Competency project get?

146. Business analysis scope?

147. How do you know that you have done this right?

148. How will you communicate scheduled tasks to other team members?

149. How will the requirements become prioritized?

2.4 Requirements Documentation: Architecture Competency

150. Are there legal issues?

151. What kind of entity is a problem ?

152. Who provides requirements?

153. Consistency. are there any requirements conflicts?

154. What is the risk associated with cost and schedule?

155. Is the requirement properly understood?

156. How will they be documented / shared?

157. Validity. does the system provide the functions which best support the customers needs?

158. How much testing do you need to do to prove that your system is safe?

159. How do you know when a Requirement is accurate enough?

160. Completeness. are all functions required by the customer included?

161. Is the requirement realistically testable?

162. How do you get the user to tell you what they want?

163. What happens when requirements are wrong?

164. Can the requirements be checked?

165. How can you document system requirements?

166. If applicable; are there issues linked with the fact that this is an offshore Architecture Competency project?

167. Where do system and software requirements come from, what are sources?

168. What will be the integration problems?

169. What facilities must be supported by the system?

2.5 Requirements Traceability Matrix: Architecture Competency

170. How do you manage scope?

171. What is the WBS?

172. Why do you manage scope?

173. How will it affect the stakeholders personally in career?

174. Describe the process for approving requirements so they can be added to the traceability matrix and Architecture Competency project work can be performed. Will the Architecture Competency project requirements become approved in writing?

175. Do you have a clear understanding of all subcontracts in place?

176. Why use a WBS?

177. What are the chronologies, contingencies, consequences, criteria?

178. What percentage of Architecture Competency projects are producing traceability matrices between requirements and other work products?

179. Is there a requirements traceability process in place?

180. Will you use a Requirements Traceability Matrix?

181. How small is small enough?

2.6 Project Scope Statement: Architecture Competency

182. Are there adequate Architecture Competency project control systems?

183. Will tasks be marked complete only after QA has been successfully completed?

184. What are the possible consequences should a risk come to occur?

185. Will the risk plan be updated on a regular and frequent basis?

186. Is an issue management process documented and filed?

187. What actions will be taken to mitigate the risk?

188. Were key Architecture Competency project stakeholders brought into the Architecture Competency project Plan?

189. Write a brief purpose statement for this Architecture Competency project. Include a business justification statement. What is the product of this Architecture Competency project?

190. Are there specific processes you will use to evaluate and approve/reject changes?

191. If you were to write a list of what should not be

included in the scope statement, what are the things that you would recommend be described as out-of-scope?

192. Were potential customers involved early in the planning process?

193. Will the qa related information be reported regularly as part of the status reporting mechanisms?

194. How often do you estimate that the scope might change, and why?

195. Are there issues that could affect the existing requirements for the result, service, or product if the scope changes?

196. Risks?

197. Elements that deal with providing the detail?

198. What is change?

199. Is there a process (test plans, inspections, reviews) defined for verifying outputs for each task?

2.7 Assumption and Constraint Log: Architecture Competency

200. Are there standards for code development?

201. How many Architecture Competency project staff does this specific process affect?

202. What strengths do you have?

203. Does the traceability documentation describe the tool and/or mechanism to be used to capture traceability throughout the life cycle?

204. Have adequate resources been provided by management to ensure Architecture Competency project success?

205. Is this model reasonable?

206. If it is out of compliance, should the process be amended or should the Plan be amended?

207. How can constraints be violated?

208. What threats might prevent you from getting there?

209. Is there adequate stakeholder participation for the vetting of requirements definition, changes and management?

210. Is the steering committee active in Architecture

Competency project oversight?

211. How relevant is this attribute to this Architecture Competency project or audit?

212. Does the plan conform to standards?

213. Are there ways to reduce the time it takes to get something approved?

214. What does an audit system look like?

215. Are there procedures in place to effectively manage interdependencies with other Architecture Competency projects / systems?

216. Is the current scope of the Architecture Competency project substantially different than that originally defined in the approved Architecture Competency project plan?

217. Are there cosmetic errors that hinder readability and comprehension?

218. Do documented requirements exist for all critical components and areas, including technical, business, interfaces, performance, security and conversion requirements?

2.8 Work Breakdown Structure: Architecture Competency

219. Why is it useful?

220. How much detail?

221. How far down?

222. What is the probability of completing the Architecture Competency project in less that xx days?

223. What has to be done?

224. How big is a work-package?

225. Is it a change in scope?

226. When do you stop?

227. Where does it take place?

228. How many levels?

229. When would you develop a Work Breakdown Structure?

230. Why would you develop a Work Breakdown Structure?

231. Who has to do it?

232. What is the probability that the Architecture

Competency project duration will exceed xx weeks?

233. When does it have to be done?

2.9 WBS Dictionary: Architecture Competency

234. Does the contractor use objective results, design reviews and tests to trace schedule performance?

235. Does the scheduling system identify in a timely manner the status of work?

236. What is wrong with this Architecture Competency project?

237. Identify and isolate causes of favorable and unfavorable cost and schedule variances?

238. Software specification, development, integration, and testing, licenses ?

239. Are management actions taken to reduce indirect costs when there are significant adverse variances?

240. Are current work performance indicators and goals relatable to original goals as modified by contractual changes, replanning, and reprogramming actions?

241. Do the lines of authority for incurring indirect costs correspond to the lines of responsibility for management control of the same components of costs?

242. What went right?

243. Are procedures established to prevent changes to the contract budget base other than the already stated authorized by contractual action?

244. Are overhead costs budgets established on a basis consistent with anticipated direct business base?

245. Are the latest revised estimates of costs at completion compared with the established budgets at appropriate levels and causes of variances identified?

246. Does the sum of all work package budgets plus planning packages within control accounts equal the budgets assigned to the already stated control accounts?

247. Are work packages assigned to performing organizations?

248. Are records maintained to show full accountability for all material purchased for the contract, including the residual inventory?

249. Are significant decision points, constraints, and interfaces identified as key milestones?

250. Is work progressively subdivided into detailed work packages as requirements are defined?

251. How detailed should a Architecture Competency project get?

252. Changes in the current direct and Architecture

Competency projected base?

253. Are estimates of costs at completion generated in a rational, consistent manner?

2.10 Schedule Management Plan: Architecture Competency

254. Has a Architecture Competency project Communications Plan been developed?

255. What is the difference between % Complete and % work?

256. Are written status reports provided on a designated frequent basis?

257. Sensitivity analysis?

258. Is there an issues management plan in place?

259. Is the quality assurance team identified?

260. Are action items captured and managed?

261. Are any non-compliance issues that exist due to your organizations practices communicated to your organization?

262. Is the critical path valid?

263. Has a provision been made to reassess Architecture Competency project risks at various Architecture Competency project stages?

264. Identify the amount of schedule variation that triggers a warning. What happens if a warning is triggered?

265. Are the results of quality assurance reviews provided to affected groups & individuals?

266. Are Architecture Competency project contact logs kept up to date?

267. Are meeting minutes captured and sent out after the meeting?

268. Has a structured approach been used to break work effort into manageable components (WBS)?

269. Are tasks tracked by hours?

270. Define units of measurement for each resource. For example, are you referencing gallons or liters?

271. Has a quality assurance plan been developed for the Architecture Competency project?

272. Are schedule performance measures defined including pre-set triggers for specific actions?

2.11 Activity List: Architecture Competency

273. When do the individual activities need to start and finish?

274. What are the critical bottleneck activities?

275. How do you determine the late start (LS) for each activity?

276. What went well?

277. How will it be performed?

278. Is there anything planned that does not need to be here?

279. The wbs is developed as part of a joint planning session. and how do you know that youhave done this right?

280. In what sequence?

281. When will the work be performed?

282. What are you counting on?

283. What is the probability the Architecture Competency project can be completed in xx weeks?

284. What is your organizations history in doing similar activities?

285. What is the total time required to complete the Architecture Competency project if no delays occur?

286. Should you include sub-activities?

287. Are the required resources available or need to be acquired?

288. What is the LF and LS for each activity?

289. Who will perform the work?

290. How can the Architecture Competency project be displayed graphically to better visualize the activities?

2.12 Activity Attributes: Architecture Competency

291. Activity: what is Missing?

292. Were there other ways you could have organized the data to achieve similar results?

293. What is missing?

294. What is the general pattern here?

295. Is there a trend during the year?

296. Have you identified the Activity Leveling Priority code value on each activity?

297. Has management defined a definite timeframe for the turnaround or Architecture Competency project window?

298. Which method produces the more accurate cost assignment?

299. Would you consider either of corresponding activities an outlier?

300. How many days do you need to complete the work scope with a limit of X number of resources?

301. Have constraints been applied to the start and finish milestones for the phases?

302. Time for overtime?

303. Resource is assigned to?

304. Where else does it apply?

305. Resources to accomplish the work?

306. How many resources do you need to complete the work scope within a limit of X number of days?

2.13 Milestone List: Architecture Competency

307. How do you manage time?

308. Global influences?

309. Usps (unique selling points)?

310. Can you derive how soon can the whole Architecture Competency project finish?

311. What is the market for your technology, product or service?

312. How late can the activity finish?

313. New USPs?

314. What would happen if a delivery of material was one week late?

315. How soon can the activity start?

316. How late can the activity start?

317. Legislative effects?

318. Political effects?

319. Gaps in capabilities?

320. Sustaining internal capabilities?

321. Continuity, supply chain robustness?

322. Which path is the critical path?

323. Describe the industry you are in and the market growth opportunities. What is the market for your technology, product or service?

324. How will the milestone be verified?

2.14 Network Diagram: Architecture Competency

325. Exercise: what is the probability that the Architecture Competency project duration will exceed xx weeks?

326. What is the completion time?

327. Will crashing x weeks return more in benefits than it costs?

328. What job or jobs could run concurrently?

329. Where do you schedule uncertainty time?

330. What are the Key Success Factors?

331. Review the logical flow of the network diagram. Take a look at which activities you have first and then sequence the activities. Do they make sense?

332. What is the lowest cost to complete this Architecture Competency project in xx weeks?

333. Are the gantt chart and/or network diagram updated periodically and used to assess the overall Architecture Competency project timetable?

334. What can be done concurrently?

335. Can you calculate the confidence level?

336. Why must you schedule milestones, such as reviews, throughout the Architecture Competency project?

337. What job or jobs follow it?

338. If a current contract exists, can you provide the vendor name, contract start, and contract expiration date?

339. How difficult will it be to do specific activities on this Architecture Competency project?

340. What activities must follow this activity?

341. What is the probability of completing the Architecture Competency project in less that xx days?

342. What activity must be completed immediately before this activity can start?

343. What activities must occur simultaneously with this activity?

344. What must be completed before an activity can be started?

2.15 Activity Resource Requirements: Architecture Competency

345. How do you handle petty cash?

346. Why do you do that?

347. Other support in specific areas?

348. What is the Work Plan Standard?

349. When does monitoring begin?

350. What are constraints that you might find during the Human Resource Planning process?

351. How many signatures do you require on a check and does this match what is in your policy and procedures?

352. Which logical relationship does the PDM use most often?

353. Are there unresolved issues that need to be addressed?

354. Organizational Applicability?

355. Anything else?

356. Do you use tools like decomposition and rolling-wave planning to produce the activity list and other outputs?

2.16 Resource Breakdown Structure: Architecture Competency

357. Which resource planning tool provides information on resource responsibility and accountability?

358. What is the primary purpose of the human resource plan?

359. Who is allowed to see what data about which resources?

360. How should the information be delivered?

361. What are the requirements for resource data?

362. Who is allowed to perform which functions?

363. How difficult will it be to do specific activities on this Architecture Competency project?

364. Is predictive resource analysis being done?

365. Who needs what information?

366. What is the number one predictor of a groups productivity?

367. What can you do to improve productivity?

368. The list could probably go on, but, the thing that you would most like to know is, How long & How

much?

369. Who delivers the information?

370. When do they need the information?

371. Who will use the system?

372. Are the required resources available?

373. Who will be used as a Architecture Competency project team member?

2.17 Activity Duration Estimates: Architecture Competency

374. Which type of mathematical analysis is being used?

375. Which is correct?

376. What is the duration of a milestone?

377. Total slack can be calculated by which equations?

378. Who will provide inputs for it?

379. What are some general rules of thumb for deciding if cost variance, schedule variance, cost performance index, and schedule performance index numbers are good or bad?

380. What questions do you have about the sample documents provided?

381. What tasks can take place concurrently?

382. Are Architecture Competency project records organized, maintained, and assessable by Architecture Competency project team members?

383. Will the new application be developed using existing hardware, software, and networks?

384. Does a process exist to determine the potential loss or gain if risk events occur?

385. After how many days will the lease cost be the same as the purchase cost for the equipment?

386. Why is it difficult to use Architecture Competency project management software well?

387. Is the cost performance monitored to identify variances from the plan?

388. What does it mean to take a systems view of a Architecture Competency project?

389. What are the largest companies that provide information technology outsourcing services?

390. Are expert judgment and historical information utilized to estimate activity duration?

391. Have most organizations benefited from outsourcing?

392. How can software assist in procuring goods and services?

2.18 Duration Estimating Worksheet: Architecture Competency

393. What is an Average Architecture Competency project?

394. Value pocket identification & quantification what are value pockets?

395. What questions do you have?

396. Define the work as completely as possible. What work will be included in the Architecture Competency project?

397. What is cost and Architecture Competency project cost management?

398. Why estimate time and cost?

399. Why estimate costs?

400. What utility impacts are there?

401. How can the Architecture Competency project be displayed graphically to better visualize the activities?

402. What is the total time required to complete the Architecture Competency project if no delays occur?

403. Is this operation cost effective?

404. Will the Architecture Competency project collaborate with the local community and leverage resources?

405. Done before proceeding with this activity or what can be done concurrently?

406. What work will be included in the Architecture Competency project?

407. What info is needed?

408. Science = process: remember the scientific method?

409. What is your role?

2.19 Project Schedule: Architecture Competency

410. Your best shot for providing estimations how complex/how much work does the activity require?

411. Are key risk mitigation strategies added to the Architecture Competency project schedule?

412. Is infrastructure setup part of your Architecture Competency project?

413. To what degree is do you feel the entire team was committed to the Architecture Competency project schedule?

414. Did the Architecture Competency project come in on schedule?

415. Is the Architecture Competency project schedule available for all Architecture Competency project team members to review?

416. Eliminate unnecessary activities. Are there activities that came from a template or previous Architecture Competency project that are not applicable on this phase of this Architecture Competency project?

417. Did the Architecture Competency project come in under budget?

418. What is the difference?

419. What does that mean?

420. What is the purpose of a Architecture Competency project schedule?

421. Are the original Architecture Competency project schedule and budget realistic?

422. If there are any qualifying green components to this Architecture Competency project, what portion of the total Architecture Competency project cost is green?

423. Your Architecture Competency project management plan results in a Architecture Competency project schedule that is too long. If the Architecture Competency project network diagram cannot change and you have extra personnel resources, what is the BEST thing to do?

424. What is the most mis-scheduled part of process?

425. If you can not fix it, how do you do it differently?

426. How much slack is available in the Architecture Competency project?

427. Why do you need to manage Architecture Competency project Risk?

428. How does a Architecture Competency project get to be a year late ?

2.20 Cost Management Plan: Architecture Competency

429. Have reserves been created to address risks?

430. What is an Acceptance Management Process?

431. Are all payments made according to the contract(s)?

432. Responsibilities – what is the split of responsibilities between the owner and contractors?

433. Was the Architecture Competency project schedule reviewed by all stakeholders and formally accepted?

434. Is documentation created for communication with the suppliers and Vendors?

435. Is your organization certified as a supplier, wholesaler and/or regular dealer?

436. Have the key functions and capabilities been defined and assigned to each release or iteration?

437. Schedule contingency – how will the schedule contingency be administrated?

438. Are changes in scope (deliverable commitments) agreed to by all affected groups & individuals?

439. Has the schedule been baselined?

440. Does the resource management plan include a personnel development plan?

441. Who should write the PEP?

442. Scope of work – What is the likelihood and extent of potential future changes to the Architecture Competency project scope?

443. Are the schedule estimates reasonable given the Architecture Competency project?

444. Forecasts – how will the time and resources needed to complete the Architecture Competency project be forecast?

445. Schedule preparation – how will the schedules be prepared during each phase of the Architecture Competency project?

446. Are metrics used to evaluate and manage Vendors?

447. Is a payment system in place with proper reviews and approvals?

2.21 Activity Cost Estimates: Architecture Competency

448. What is the estimators estimating history?

449. Can you delete activities or make them inactive?

450. How do you treat administrative costs in the activity inventory?

451. How Award?

452. Will you use any tools, such as Architecture Competency project management software, to assist in capturing Earned Value metrics?

453. What do you want to know about the stay to know if costs were inappropriately high or low?

454. What is the activity recast of the budget?

455. Were the tasks or work products prepared by the consultant useful?

456. How difficult will it be to do specific tasks on the Architecture Competency project?

457. Can you change your activities?

458. Who determines when the contractor is paid?

459. How do you allocate indirect costs to activities?

460. How do you fund change orders?

461. What is the activity inventory?

462. What happens if you cannot produce the documentation for the single audit?

463. Does the estimator have experience?

464. What areas does the group agree are the biggest success on the Architecture Competency project?

465. What defines a successful Architecture Competency project?

466. Estimated cost?

2.22 Cost Estimating Worksheet: Architecture Competency

467. How will the results be shared and to whom?

468. What additional Architecture Competency project(s) could be initiated as a result of this Architecture Competency project?

469. What is the purpose of estimating?

470. What costs are to be estimated?

471. Identify the timeframe necessary to monitor progress and collect data to determine how the selected measure has changed?

472. What is the estimated labor cost today based upon this information?

473. What will others want?

474. Does the Architecture Competency project provide innovative ways for stakeholders to overcome obstacles or deliver better outcomes?

475. Ask: are others positioned to know, are others credible, and will others cooperate?

476. What happens to any remaining funds not used?

477. Is it feasible to establish a control group arrangement?

478. Who is best positioned to know and assist in identifying corresponding factors?

479. What can be included?

480. Will the Architecture Competency project collaborate with the local community and leverage resources?

481. Is the Architecture Competency project responsive to community need?

482. Can a trend be established from historical performance data on the selected measure and are the criteria for using trend analysis or forecasting methods met?

2.23 Cost Baseline: Architecture Competency

483. What do you want to measure ?

484. What is the reality?

485. Has the Architecture Competency project documentation been archived or otherwise disposed as described in the Architecture Competency project communication plan?

486. Are you asking management for something as a result of this update?

487. What does a good WBS NOT look like?

488. What is cost and Architecture Competency project cost management?

489. Has the Architecture Competency projected annual cost to operate and maintain the product(s) or service(s) been approved and funded?

490. Are procedures defined by which the cost baseline may be changed?

491. On budget?

492. Review your risk triggers -have your risks changed?

493. Impact to environment?

494. Is request in line with priorities?

495. What is the most important thing to do next to make your Architecture Competency project successful?

496. Architecture Competency project goals -should others be reconsidered?

497. Have all approved changes to the Architecture Competency project requirement been identified and impact on the performance, cost, and schedule baselines documented?

498. Who will use corresponding metrics ?

499. Will the Architecture Competency project fail if the change request is not executed?

500. What is your organizations history in doing similar tasks?

2.24 Quality Management Plan: Architecture Competency

501. Who is responsible?

502. Do you keep back-up copies of any data?

503. What are your organizations key processes (product, service, business, and support)?

504. What are you trying to accomplish?

505. Have all involved stakeholders and work groups committed to the Architecture Competency project?

506. Does the system design reflect the requirements?

507. Do trained quality assurance auditors conduct the audits as defined in the Quality Management Plan and scheduled by the Architecture Competency project manager?

508. After observing execution of process, is it in compliance with the documented Plan?

509. How are corresponding standards measured?

510. Who gets results of work?

511. Sampling part of task?

512. You know what your customers expectations are regarding this process?

513. What procedures are used to determine if you use, and the number of split, replicate or duplicate samples taken at a site?

514. How do you measure?

515. Is a component/condition present?

516. Does the Architecture Competency project have a formal Architecture Competency project Plan?

517. How are changes recorded?

518. What methods are used?

519. Have all stakeholders been identified?

2.25 Quality Metrics: Architecture Competency

520. Where is quality now?

521. What makes a visualization memorable?

522. Are quality metrics defined?

523. Are interface issues coordinated?

524. Product Availability ?

525. Is material complete (and does it meet the standards)?

526. What does this tell us?

527. Is a risk containment plan in place?

528. What if the biggest risk to your business were the already stated people who do not complain?

529. How do you know if everyone is trying to improve the right things?

530. If the defect rate during testing is substantially higher than that of the previous release (or a similar product), then ask: Did you plan for and actually improve testing effectiveness?

531. What is the timeline to meet your goal?

532. Have alternatives been defined in the event that failure occurs?

533. Are documents on hand to provide explanations of privacy and confidentiality?

534. Do you stratify metrics by product or site?

535. Subjective quality component: customer satisfaction, how do you measure it?

536. What can manufacturing professionals do to ensure quality is seen as an integral part of the entire product lifecycle?

537. There are many reasons to shore up quality-related metrics, and what metrics are important?

538. Which report did you use to create the data you are submitting?

539. Is there a set of procedures to capture, analyze and act on quality metrics?

2.26 Process Improvement Plan: Architecture Competency

540. Where do you focus?

541. Does explicit definition of the measures exist?

542. Have the supporting tools been developed or acquired?

543. What personnel are the sponsors for that initiative?

544. What is quality and how will you ensure it?

545. Purpose of goal: the motive is determined by asking, why do you want to achieve this goal?

546. What personnel are the coaches for your initiative?

547. Does your process ensure quality?

548. Are there forms and procedures to collect and record the data?

549. Are you making progress on the goals?

550. Are you making progress on your improvement plan?

551. Has a process guide to collect the data been developed?

552. What personnel are the champions for the initiative?

553. To elicit goal statements, do you ask a question such as, What do you want to achieve?

554. What is the test-cycle concept?

555. The motive is determined by asking, Why do you want to achieve this goal?

556. What actions are needed to address the problems and achieve the goals?

557. Are you meeting the quality standards?

558. Where do you want to be?

559. Are you following the quality standards?

2.27 Responsibility Assignment Matrix: Architecture Competency

560. Architecture Competency projected economic escalation?

561. What does wbs accomplish?

562. How many people do you need?

563. Competencies and craftsmanship – what competencies are necessary and what level?

564. Not any rs, as, or cs: if an identified role is only informed, should others be eliminated from the matrix?

565. Are indirect costs accumulated for comparison with the corresponding budgets?

566. Are the requirements for all items of overhead established by rational, traceable processes?

567. Availability – will the group or the person be available within the necessary time interval?

568. Are all elements of indirect expense identified to overhead cost budgets of Architecture Competency projections?

569. What is the purpose of assigning and documenting responsibility?

570. Are too many reports done in writing instead of verbally?

571. Major functional areas of contract effort?

572. Evaluate the performance of operating organizations?

573. Performance to date and material commitment?

574. What do you do when people do not respond?

575. How do you assist them to be as productive as possible?

576. Will too many Signing-off responsibilities delay the completion of the activity/deliverable?

577. Contemplated overhead expenditure for each period based on the best information currently available?

578. Are detailed work packages planned as far in advance as practicable?

2.28 Roles and Responsibilities: Architecture Competency

579. Required skills, knowledge, experience?

580. Are governance roles and responsibilities documented?

581. Are the quality assurance functions and related roles and responsibilities clearly defined?

582. Accountabilities: what are the roles and responsibilities of individual team members?

583. What should you do now to ensure that you are exceeding expectations and excelling in your current position?

584. Who is involved?

585. Does the team have access to and ability to use data analysis tools?

586. Is there a training program in place for stakeholders covering expectations, roles and responsibilities and any addition knowledge others need to be good stakeholders?

587. What is working well within your organizations performance management system?

588. Once the responsibilities are defined for the Architecture Competency project, have the

deliverables, roles and responsibilities been clearly communicated to every participant?

589. What is working well?

590. Do you take the time to clearly define roles and responsibilities on Architecture Competency project tasks?

591. What expectations were met?

592. Are Architecture Competency project team roles and responsibilities identified and documented?

593. Was the expectation clearly communicated?

594. What expectations were NOT met?

595. Are your policies supportive of a culture of quality data?

596. Implementation of actions: Who are the responsible units?

597. What should you do now to prepare for your career 5+ years from now?

598. What should you highlight for improvement?

2.29 Human Resource Management Plan: Architecture Competency

599. Are staff skills known and available for each task?

600. Has a sponsor been identified?

601. Was your organizations estimating methodology being used and followed?

602. Is Architecture Competency project status reviewed with the steering and executive teams at appropriate intervals?

603. Pareto diagrams, statistical sampling, flow charting or trend analysis used quality monitoring?

604. Do Architecture Competency project teams & team members report on status / activities / progress?

605. How will the Architecture Competency project manage expectations & meet needs and requirements?

606. Is the manpower level sufficient to meet the future business requirements?

607. Was the Architecture Competency project schedule reviewed by all stakeholders and formally accepted?

608. Are there dependencies with other initiatives or Architecture Competency projects?

609. Are software metrics formally captured, analyzed and used as a basis for other Architecture Competency project estimates?

610. Is the current culture aligned with the vision, mission, and values of the department?

611. Are internal Architecture Competency project status meetings held at reasonable intervals?

612. Is there a requirements change management processes in place?

613. Have all involved Architecture Competency project stakeholders and work groups committed to the Architecture Competency project?

614. Are Architecture Competency project team roles and responsibilities identified and documented?

615. Are issues raised, assessed, actioned, and resolved in a timely and efficient manner?

616. Were the budget estimates reasonable?

2.30 Communications Management Plan: Architecture Competency

617. Who were proponents/opponents?

618. Are you constantly rushing from meeting to meeting?

619. Will messages be directly related to the release strategy or phases of the Architecture Competency project?

620. What approaches to you feel are the best ones to use?

621. Who will use or be affected by the result of a Architecture Competency project?

622. Are others needed?

623. Who did you turn to if you had questions?

624. Do you feel more overwhelmed by stakeholders?

625. What data is going to be required?

626. Do you feel a register helps?

627. Who needs to know and how much?

628. Who have you worked with in past, similar initiatives?

629. What is the stakeholders level of authority?

630. What are the interrelationships?

631. Can you think of other people who might have concerns or interests?

632. What to know?

633. How were corresponding initiatives successful?

634. How did the term stakeholder originate?

635. Do you then often overlook a key stakeholder or stakeholder group?

2.31 Risk Management Plan: Architecture Competency

636. How do you manage Architecture Competency project Risk?

637. How is implementation of risk actions performed?

638. Why do you want risk management?

639. Are end-users enthusiastically committed to the Architecture Competency project and the system/product to be built?

640. Which risks should get the attention?

641. Are status updates being made on schedule and are the updates clearly described?

642. Are Architecture Competency project requirements stable?

643. Does the software engineering team have the right mix of skills?

644. Risk may be made during which step of risk management?

645. What things might go wrong?

646. Are the software tools integrated with each other?

647. Do the people have the right combinations of skills?

648. Workarounds are determined during which step of risk management?

649. Financial risk -can your organization afford to undertake the Architecture Competency project?

650. What are the chances the event will occur?

651. Risk categories: what are the main categories of risks that should be addressed on this Architecture Competency project?

652. Is a software Architecture Competency project management tool available?

653. What are the cost, schedule and resource impacts if the risk does occur?

654. Are the reports useful and easy to read?

655. Have customers been involved fully in the definition of requirements?

2.32 Risk Register: Architecture Competency

656. Is further information required before making a decision?

657. What is the appropriate level of risk management for this Architecture Competency project?

658. What are the main aims, objectives of the policy, strategy, or service and the intended outcomes?

659. Can the likelihood and impact of failing to achieve corresponding recommendations and action plans be assessed?

660. Have other controls and solutions been implemented in other services which could be applied as an alternative to additional funding?

661. Recovery actions - planned actions taken once a risk has occurred to allow you to move on. What should you do after?

662. What should you do now?

663. How are risks identified?

664. Severity Prediction?

665. What would the impact to the Architecture Competency project objectives be should the risk arise?

666. Are there any gaps in the evidence?

667. What could prevent you delivering on the strategic program objectives and what is being done to mitigate corresponding issues?

668. What has changed since the last period?

669. Are your objectives at risk?

670. Technology risk -is the Architecture Competency project technically feasible?

671. What should you do when?

672. Methodology: how will risk management be performed on this Architecture Competency project?

673. What is your current and future risk profile?

674. Which key risks have ineffective responses or outstanding improvement actions?

2.33 Probability and Impact Assessment: Architecture Competency

675. To what extent is the chosen technology maturing?

676. Would avoiding any of corresponding impact the Architecture Competency projects chance of success?

677. Is the customer willing to participate in reviews?

678. Has the need for the Architecture Competency project been properly established?

679. What are the uncertainties associated with the technology selected for the Architecture Competency project?

680. What are the likely future requirements?

681. Can the risk be avoided by choosing a different alternative?

682. What is the probability of the risk occurring?

683. What is the impact if the risk does occur?

684. What is the likely future demand of the customer?

685. Are the risk data timely and relevant?

686. Are the facilities, expertise, resources, and management know-how available to handle the situation?

687. What things are likely to change?

688. How would you suggest monitoring for risk transition indicators?

689. How well is the risk understood?

690. Do benefits and chances of success outweigh potential damage if success is not attained?

691. Management -what contingency plans do you have if the risk becomes a reality?

692. Do you use any methods to analyze risks?

693. What is the past performance of the Architecture Competency project manager?

2.34 Probability and Impact Matrix: Architecture Competency

694. Can it be enlarged by drawing people from other areas of your organization?

695. Are you working on the right risks?

696. Do you train all developers in the process?

697. Are compilers and code generators available and suitable for the product to be built?

698. Which should be probably done NEXT?

699. Pay attention to the quality of the plans: is the content complete, or does it seem to be lacking detail?

700. What new technologies are being explored in the same area?

701. What is the culture of the market and your organization?

702. Are staff committed for the duration of the Architecture Competency project?

703. Can you stabilize dynamic risk factors?

704. Amount of reused software?

705. Are there new risks that mitigation strategies

might introduce?

706. My Architecture Competency project leader has suddenly left your organization, what do you do?

707. How would you assess the risk management process in the Architecture Competency project?

708. What is the industrial relations prevailing in this organization?

2.35 Risk Data Sheet: Architecture Competency

709. How can it happen?

710. What is the likelihood of it happening?

711. Risk of what?

712. What can happen?

713. Has a sensitivity analysis been carried out?

714. Is the data sufficiently specified in terms of the type of failure being analyzed, and its frequency or probability?

715. Who has a vested interest in how you perform as your organization (our stakeholders)?

716. What is the chance that it will happen?

717. How do you handle product safely?

718. What are your core values?

719. What are you trying to achieve (Objectives)?

720. What is the environment within which you operate (social trends, economic, community values, broad based participation, national directions etc.)?

721. How reliable is the data source?

722. What if client refuses?

723. Type of risk identified?

724. Are new hazards created?

725. What actions can be taken to eliminate or remove risk?

726. Has the most cost-effective solution been chosen?

727. Potential for recurrence?

728. What are the main threats to your existence?

2.36 Procurement Management Plan: Architecture Competency

729. Is it possible to track all classes of Architecture Competency project work (e.g. scheduled, un-scheduled, defect repair, etc.)?

730. Are assumptions being identified, recorded, analyzed, qualified and closed?

731. Were Architecture Competency project team members involved in the development of activity & task decomposition?

732. Is there an on-going process in place to monitor Architecture Competency project risks?

733. Are meeting objectives identified for each meeting?

734. Are decisions captured in a decisions log?

735. Do you have the reasons why the changes to your organizational systems and capabilities are required?

736. Is the assigned Architecture Competency project manager a PMP (Certified Architecture Competency project manager) and experienced?

737. Financial capacity; does the seller have, or can the seller reasonably be expected to obtain, the financial resources needed?

738. Are there checklists created to determine if all quality processes are followed?

739. Is stakeholder involvement adequate?

740. Similar Architecture Competency projects?

741. Is the Architecture Competency project schedule available for all Architecture Competency project team members to review?

742. Staffing Requirements?

743. Are change requests logged and managed?

744. Are adequate resources provided for the quality assurance function?

2.37 Source Selection Criteria: Architecture Competency

745. How should oral presentations be evaluated?

746. Are considerations anticipated?

747. With the rapid changes in information technology, will media be readable in five or ten years?

748. What past performance information should be requested?

749. What should be considered when developing evaluation standards?

750. What is the last item a Architecture Competency project manager must do to finalize Architecture Competency project close-out?

751. What instructions should be provided regarding oral presentations?

752. Are evaluators ready to begin this task?

753. What information may not be provided?

754. When is it appropriate to conduct a preproposal conference?

755. What are the special considerations for preaward debriefings?

756. Can you identify proposed teaming partners and/or subcontractors and consider the nature and extent of proposed involvement in satisfying the Architecture Competency project requirements?

757. What common questions or problems are associated with debriefings?

758. How is past performance evaluated?

759. Do you consider all weaknesses, significant weaknesses, and deficiencies?

760. Are responses to considerations adequate?

761. What documentation should be used to support the selection decision?

762. Who is entitled to a debriefing?

763. What documentation is necessary regarding electronic communications?

764. What are the most common types of rating systems?

2.38 Stakeholder Management Plan: Architecture Competency

765. What methods are to be used for managing and monitoring subcontractors (eg agreements, contracts etc)?

766. Is a pmo (Architecture Competency project management office) in place and does it provide oversight to the Architecture Competency project?

767. How many Architecture Competency project staff does this specific process affect?

768. Are parking lot items captured?

769. Are stakeholders aware and supportive of the principles and practices of modern software estimation?

770. Have all necessary approvals been obtained?

771. What is to be the method of release?

772. Are software metrics formally captured, analyzed and used as a basis for other Architecture Competency project estimates?

773. Who will perform the review(s)?

774. Are formal code reviews conducted?

775. Are changes in deliverable commitments agreed

to by all affected groups & individuals?

776. Describe the process that will be used to design, develop, review, accept, distribute and change outputs. Will all outputs delivered by the Architecture Competency project follow the same process?

777. Does the Architecture Competency project have a formal Architecture Competency project Charter?

778. Has the scope management document been updated and distributed to help prevent scope creep?

779. Were Architecture Competency project team members involved in the development of activity & task decomposition?

780. Have all unresolved risks been documented?

2.39 Change Management Plan: Architecture Competency

781. Has an information & communications plan been developed?

782. Will the culture embrace or reject this change?

783. Have the business unit contacts been selected and notified?

784. How frequently should you repeat the message?

785. Who might present the most resistance?

786. Have the business unit contacts been briefed by the Architecture Competency project team?

787. Do the proposed users have access to the appropriate documentation?

788. Is there a software application relevant to this deliverable?

789. What is the worst thing that can happen if you chose not to communicate this information?

790. Have the systems been configured and tested?

791. What are the training strategies?

792. Who will be the change levers?

793. How far reaching in your organization is the change?

794. Who will fund the training?

795. What provokes organizational change?

796. What new competencies will be required for the roles?

797. Where will the funds come from?

798. What are the specific target groups / audience that will be impacted by this change?

799. Why would a Architecture Competency project run more smoothly when change management is emphasized from the beginning?

800. Who might be able to help you the most?

3.0 Executing Process Group: Architecture Competency

801. What are the critical steps involved with strategy mapping?

802. How can your organization use a weighted decision matrix to evaluate proposals as part of source selection?

803. How do you prevent staff are just doing busywork to pass the time?

804. Contingency planning. if a risk event occurs, what will you do?

805. What type of people would you want on your team?

806. What are the critical steps involved in selecting measures and initiatives?

807. How well did the team follow the chosen processes?

808. It under budget or over budget?

809. What are the main types of contracts if you do decide to outsource?

810. What areas were overlooked on this Architecture Competency project?

811. What are deliverables of your Architecture Competency project?

812. Will a new application be developed using existing hardware, software, and networks?

813. What is the difference between using brainstorming and the Delphi technique for risk identification?

814. How do you control progress of your Architecture Competency project?

815. Would you rate yourself as being risk-averse, risk-neutral, or risk-seeking?

816. How could stakeholders negatively impact your Architecture Competency project?

817. Just how important is your work to the overall success of the Architecture Competency project?

818. What does it mean to take a systems view of a Architecture Competency project?

3.1 Team Member Status Report: Architecture Competency

819. What specific interest groups do you have in place?

820. How it is to be done?

821. Does your organization have the means (staff, money, contract, etc.) to produce or to acquire the product, good, or service?

822. Are the attitudes of staff regarding Architecture Competency project work improving?

823. When a teams productivity and success depend on collaboration and the efficient flow of information, what generally fails them?

824. Are the products of your organizations Architecture Competency projects meeting customers objectives?

825. Do you have an Enterprise Architecture Competency project Management Office (EPMO)?

826. Does the product, good, or service already exist within your organization?

827. How can you make it practical?

828. Why is it to be done?

829. Does every department have to have a Architecture Competency project Manager on staff?

830. Will the staff do training or is that done by a third party?

831. How will resource planning be done?

832. Are your organizations Architecture Competency projects more successful over time?

833. How much risk is involved?

834. The problem with Reward & Recognition Programs is that the truly deserving people all too often get left out. How can you make it practical?

835. Is there evidence that staff is taking a more professional approach toward management of your organizations Architecture Competency projects?

836. What is to be done?

837. How does this product, good, or service meet the needs of the Architecture Competency project and your organization as a whole?

3.2 Change Request: Architecture Competency

838. Describe how modifications, enhancements, defects and/or deficiencies shall be notified (e.g. Problem Reports, Change Requests etc) and managed. Detail warranty and/or maintenance periods?

839. How do team members communicate with each other?

840. Are there requirements attributes that are strongly related to the occurrence of defects and failures?

841. Is it feasible to use requirements attributes as predictors of reliability?

842. Who is responsible to authorize changes?

843. How to get changes (code) out in a timely manner?

844. Who is included in the change control team?

845. Since there are no change requests in your Architecture Competency project at this point, what must you have before you begin?

846. How is the change documented (format, content, storage)?

847. How do you get changes (code) out in a timely manner?

848. Who can suggest changes?

849. How can changes be graded?

850. What mechanism is used to appraise others of changes that are made?

851. Will all change requests and current status be logged?

852. What are the Impacts to your organization?

853. What are the basic mechanics of the Change Advisory Board (CAB)?

854. How shall the implementation of changes be recorded?

855. What are the requirements for urgent changes?

856. How are changes graded and who is responsible for the rating?

3.3 Change Log: Architecture Competency

857. How does this change affect scope?

858. Will the Architecture Competency project fail if the change request is not executed?

859. Does the suggested change request represent a desired enhancement to the products functionality?

860. When was the request submitted?

861. Does the suggested change request seem to represent a necessary enhancement to the product?

862. Is the requested change request a result of changes in other Architecture Competency project(s)?

863. Where do changes come from?

864. Who initiated the change request?

865. Is the change request open, closed or pending?

866. Is the submitted change a new change or a modification of a previously approved change?

867. Do the described changes impact on the integrity or security of the system?

868. Is the change backward compatible without limitations?

869. How does this relate to the standards developed for specific business processes?

870. When was the request approved?

871. Should a more thorough impact analysis be conducted?

872. Is the change request within Architecture Competency project scope?

873. How does this change affect the timeline of the schedule?

874. Is this a mandatory replacement?

3.4 Decision Log: Architecture Competency

875. Linked to original objective?

876. Decision-making process; how will the team make decisions?

877. Does anything need to be adjusted?

878. At what point in time does loss become unacceptable?

879. How does provision of information, both in terms of content and presentation, influence acceptance of alternative strategies?

880. Which variables make a critical difference?

881. What was the rationale for the decision?

882. Who will be given a copy of this document and where will it be kept?

883. How do you know when you are achieving it?

884. Do strategies and tactics aimed at less than full control reduce the costs of management or simply shift the cost burden?

885. Adversarial environment. is your opponent open to a non-traditional workflow, or will it likely challenge anything you do?

886. What makes you different or better than others companies selling the same thing?

887. With whom was the decision shared or considered?

888. What is the line where eDiscovery ends and document review begins?

889. It becomes critical to track and periodically revisit both operational effectiveness; Are you noticing all that you need to, and are you interpreting what you see effectively?

890. Meeting purpose; why does this team meet?

891. What is the average size of your matters in an applicable measurement?

892. How do you define success?

893. What alternatives/risks were considered?

894. Is everything working as expected?

3.5 Quality Audit: Architecture Competency

895. What has changed/improved as a result of the review processes?

896. How does your organization ensure that equipment is appropriately maintained and producing valid results?

897. Is the reports overall tone appropriate?

898. How does your organization know that its Mission, Vision and Values Statements are appropriate and effectively guiding your organization?

899. How does your organization know that its teaching activities (and staff learning) are effectively and constructively enhanced by its activities?

900. If your organization thinks it is doing something well, can it prove this?

901. Are the review comments incorporated?

902. How does your organization know that its system for attending to the particular needs of its international staff is appropriately effective and constructive?

903. Do all staff have the necessary authority and resources to deliver what is expected of them?

904. What are you trying to do?

905. Is quality audit a prerequisite for program accreditation or program recognition?

906. Are adequate and conveniently located toilet facilities available for use by the employees?

907. How does your organization know that its staff entrance standards are appropriately effective and constructive and being implemented consistently?

908. How does your organization know that it is maintaining a conducive staff climate?

909. What are your supplier audits?

910. What does the organizarion look for in a Quality audit?

911. How does your organization know that its support services planning and management systems are appropriately effective and constructive?

912. How does your organization know that its information technology system is serving its needs as effectively and constructively as is appropriate?

913. Are the intentions consistent with external obligations (such as applicable laws)?

914. How does your organization know that its staff have appropriate access to a fair and effective grievance process?

3.6 Team Directory: Architecture Competency

915. When does information need to be distributed?

916. Who are the Team Members?

917. Why is the work necessary?

918. When will you produce deliverables?

919. Process decisions: are there any statutory or regulatory issues relevant to the timely execution of work?

920. Process decisions: how well was task order work performed?

921. Decisions: is the most suitable form of contract being used?

922. Decisions: what could be done better to improve the quality of the constructed product?

923. Where will the product be used and/or delivered or built when appropriate?

924. Days from the time the issue is identified?

925. Process decisions: is work progressing on schedule and per contract requirements?

926. Contract requirements complied with?

927. Who will report Architecture Competency project status to all stakeholders?

928. Is construction on schedule?

929. Who will write the meeting minutes and distribute?

930. How does the team resolve conflicts and ensure tasks are completed?

931. How will the team handle changes?

932. Process decisions: do job conditions warrant additional actions to collect job information and document on-site activity?

933. Who will talk to the customer?

934. What are you going to deliver or accomplish?

3.7 Team Operating Agreement: Architecture Competency

935. Do you upload presentation materials in advance and test the technology?

936. Are leadership responsibilities shared among team members (versus a single leader)?

937. Do you ensure that all participants know how to use the required technology?

938. Are there more than two national cultures represented by your team?

939. Do you solicit member feedback about meetings and what would make them better?

940. What is culture?

941. How will group handle unplanned absences?

942. Do you leverage technology engagement tools group chat, polls, screen sharing, etc.?

943. What is group supervision?

944. Have you set the goals and objectives of the team?

945. What are the current caseload numbers in the unit?

946. What resources can be provided for the team in terms of equipment, space, time for training, protected time and space for meetings, and travel allowances?

947. Communication protocols: how will the team communicate?

948. Have you established procedures that team members can follow to work effectively together, such as a team operating agreement?

949. Do you prevent individuals from dominating the meeting?

950. Are there more than two native languages represented by your team?

951. Resource allocation: how will individual team members account for time and expenses, and how will this be allocated in the team budget?

952. Why does your organization want to participate in teaming?

953. Do you ask participants to close laptops and place mobile devices on silent on the table while the meeting is in progress?

954. What are some potential sources of conflict among team members?

3.8 Team Performance Assessment: Architecture Competency

955. To what degree do members understand and articulate the same purpose without relying on ambiguous abstractions?

956. To what degree are fresh input and perspectives systematically caught and added (for example, through information and analysis, new members, and senior sponsors)?

957. To what degree do team members feel that the purpose of the team is important, if not exciting?

958. To what degree does the teams purpose constitute a broader, deeper aspiration than just accomplishing short-term goals?

959. How do you encourage members to learn from each other?

960. To what degree does the team possess adequate membership to achieve its ends?

961. How hard do you try to make a good selection?

962. To what degree are the members clear on what they are individually responsible for and what they are jointly responsible for?

963. What do you think is the most constructive thing that could be done now to resolve considerations and

disputes about method variance?

964. To what degree are the goals realistic?

965. If you have criticized someones work for method variance in your role as reviewer, what was the circumstance?

966. To what degree does the teams work approach provide opportunity for members to engage in results-based evaluation?

967. Individual task proficiency and team process behavior: what is important for team functioning?

968. Social categorization and intergroup behaviour: Does minimal intergroup discrimination make social identity more positive?

969. To what degree can team members frequently and easily communicate with one another?

970. To what degree are the relative importance and priority of the goals clear to all team members?

971. How much interpersonal friction is there in your team?

972. To what degree can all members engage in open and interactive considerations?

973. What is method variance?

974. To what degree will the team adopt a concrete, clearly understood, and agreed-upon approach that will result in achievement of the teams goals?

3.9 Team Member Performance Assessment: Architecture Competency

975. What does collaboration look like?

976. To what degree can team members meet frequently enough to accomplish the teams ends?

977. What is the Business Management Oversight Process?

978. To what degree do team members articulate the teams work approach?

979. To what extent did the evaluation influence the instructional path, such as with adaptive testing?

980. What is the role of the Reviewer?

981. What is collaboration?

982. Is it critical or vital to the job?

983. Are the goals SMART ?

984. Who receives a benchmark visit?

985. How will they be formed?

986. How do you currently account for your results in the teams achievement?

987. Does adaptive training work?

988. What is the large, desired outcome?

989. How should adaptive assessments be implemented?

990. Does the rater (supervisor) have to wait for the interim or final performance assessment review to tell an employee that the employees performance is unsatisfactory?

991. What happens if a team member receives a Rating of Unsatisfactory?

992. To what degree do team members understand one anothers roles and skills?

3.10 Issue Log: Architecture Competency

993. In classifying stakeholders, which approach to do so are you using?

994. Are they needed?

995. Are stakeholder roles recognized by your organization?

996. Who reported the issue?

997. Do you prepare stakeholder engagement plans?

998. What would have to change?

999. How often do you engage with stakeholders?

1000. Who is the issue assigned to?

1001. How do you reply to this question; you am new here and managing this major program. How do you suggest you build your network?

1002. Why do you manage communications?

1003. What is the status of the issue?

1004. Who do you turn to if you have questions?

1005. Are there potential barriers between the team and the stakeholder?

1006. Why multiple evaluators?

1007. Persistence; will users learn a work around or will they be bothered every time?

1008. What help do you and your team need from the stakeholders?

1009. What is the impact on the risks?

1010. Which stakeholders are thought leaders, influences, or early adopters?

1011. Who is involved as you identify stakeholders?

4.0 Monitoring and Controlling Process Group: Architecture Competency

1012. Change, where should you look for problems?

1013. What areas were overlooked on this Architecture Competency project?

1014. How well did the chosen processes fit the needs of the Architecture Competency project?

1015. Who are the Architecture Competency project stakeholders?

1016. If a risk event occurs, what will you do?

1017. In what way has the program come up with innovative measures for problem-solving?

1018. What areas does the group agree are the biggest success on the Architecture Competency project?

1019. How to ensure validity, quality and consistency?

1020. What departments are involved in its daily operation?

1021. What resources are necessary?

1022. What is the timeline for the Architecture Competency project?

1023. Are the services being delivered?

1024. What are the goals of the program?

1025. Is the verbiage used appropriate and understandable?

1026. What factors are contributing to progress or delay in the achievement of products and results?

1027. Were sponsors and decision makers available when needed outside regularly scheduled meetings?

1028. Do the products created live up to the necessary quality?

1029. Overall, how does the program function to serve the clients?

1030. What resources (both financial and non-financial) are available/needed?

4.1 Project Performance Report: Architecture Competency

1031. To what degree does the informal organization make use of individual resources and meet individual needs?

1032. To what degree are the demands of the task compatible with and converge with the mission and functions of the formal organization?

1033. To what degree are the teams goals and objectives clear, simple, and measurable?

1034. To what degree is there a sense that only the team can succeed?

1035. To what degree does the formal organization make use of individual resources and meet individual needs?

1036. To what degree do the goals specify concrete team work products?

1037. To what degree will the approach capitalize on and enhance the skills of all team members in a manner that takes into consideration other demands on members of the team?

1038. To what degree are the skill areas critical to team performance present?

1039. How is the data used?

1040. To what degree can the cognitive capacity of individuals accommodate the flow of information?

1041. To what degree do individual skills and abilities match task demands?

1042. To what degree can the team ensure that all members are individually and jointly accountable for the teams purpose, goals, approach, and work-products?

1043. To what degree does the teams approach to its work allow for modification and improvement over time?

1044. What degree are the relative importance and priority of the goals clear to all team members?

1045. To what degree do the relationships of the informal organization motivate taskrelevant behavior and facilitate task completion?

1046. To what degree do team members agree with the goals, relative importance, and the ways in which achievement will be measured?

4.2 Variance Analysis: Architecture Competency

1047. How do you manage changes in the nature of the overhead requirements?

1048. How have the setting and use of standards changed over time?

1049. What does a favorable labor efficiency variance mean?

1050. Are material costs reported within the same period as that in which BCWP is earned for that material?

1051. Does the accounting system provide a basis for auditing records of direct costs chargeable to the contract?

1052. How does your organization allocate the cost of shared expenses and services?

1053. Do you identify potential or actual budget-based and time-based schedule variances?

1054. The anticipated business volume?

1055. Can process improvements lead to unfavorable variances?

1056. Is budgeted cost for work performed calculated in a manner consistent with the way work is planned?

1057. Is work properly classified as measured effort, LOE, or apportioned effort and appropriately separated?

1058. Are the bases and rates for allocating costs from each indirect pool consistently applied?

1059. What are the actual costs to date?

1060. What is the performance to date and material commitment?

1061. Are your organizations and items of cost assigned to each pool identified?

1062. What business event caused the fluctuation?

1063. What costs are avoidable if one or more customers are dropped?

4.3 Earned Value Status: Architecture Competency

1064. Where is evidence-based earned value in your organization reported?

1065. Verification is a process of ensuring that the developed system satisfies the stakeholders agreements and specifications; Are you building the product right? What do you verify?

1066. Validation is a process of ensuring that the developed system will actually achieve the stakeholders desired outcomes; Are you building the right product? What do you validate?

1067. How does this compare with other Architecture Competency projects?

1068. If earned value management (EVM) is so good in determining the true status of a Architecture Competency project and Architecture Competency project its completion, why is it that hardly any one uses it in information systems related Architecture Competency projects?

1069. Earned value can be used in almost any Architecture Competency project situation and in almost any Architecture Competency project environment. it may be used on large Architecture Competency projects, medium sized Architecture Competency projects, tiny Architecture Competency projects (in cut-down form), complex and simple

Architecture Competency projects and in any market sector. some people, of course, know all about earned value, they have used it for years - but perhaps not as effectively as they could have?

1070. What is the unit of forecast value?

1071. When is it going to finish?

1072. Where are your problem areas?

1073. Are you hitting your Architecture Competency projects targets?

1074. How much is it going to cost by the finish?

4.4 Risk Audit: Architecture Competency

1075. Which assets are important?

1076. Level of preparation and skill?

1077. Has risk management been considered when planning an event?

1078. Are enough people available?

1079. Does your auditor understand your business?

1080. Are all programs planned and conducted according to recognized safety standards?

1081. Are formal technical reviews part of this process?

1082. Do you meet all obligations relating to funds secured from grants, loans and sponsors?

1083. Do staff understand the extent of duty of care?

1084. What are the risks that could stop you from achieving your objectives?

1085. Is your organization able to present documentary evidence in support of compliance?

1086. Are procedures developed to respond to foreseeable emergencies and communicated to all involved?

1087. Do all coaches/instructors/leaders have appropriate and current accreditation?

1088. Does your organization have a social media policy and procedure?

1089. Do you have an understanding of insurance claims processes?

1090. Estimated size of product in number of programs, files, transactions?

1091. Are audit program plans risk-adjusted?

1092. Have all involved been advised of any obligations they have to sponsors?

1093. What are the outcomes you are looking for?

4.5 Contractor Status Report: Architecture Competency

1094. Are there contractual transfer concerns?

1095. Describe how often regular updates are made to the proposed solution. Are corresponding regular updates included in the standard maintenance plan?

1096. What process manages the contracts?

1097. How does the proposed individual meet each requirement?

1098. Who can list a Architecture Competency project as organization experience, your organization or a previous employee of your organization?

1099. What was the final actual cost?

1100. What was the overall budget or estimated cost?

1101. How is risk transferred?

1102. What are the minimum and optimal bandwidth requirements for the proposed solution?

1103. What was the actual budget or estimated cost for your organizations services?

1104. What is the average response time for answering a support call?

1105. If applicable; describe your standard schedule for new software version releases. Are new software version releases included in the standard maintenance plan?

1106. How long have you been using the services?

1107. What was the budget or estimated cost for your organizations services?

4.6 Formal Acceptance: Architecture Competency

1108. Was the Architecture Competency project managed well?

1109. What are the requirements against which to test, Who will execute?

1110. Do you perform formal acceptance or burn-in tests?

1111. Is formal acceptance of the Architecture Competency project product documented and distributed?

1112. Was the client satisfied with the Architecture Competency project results?

1113. General estimate of the costs and times to complete the Architecture Competency project?

1114. Did the Architecture Competency project manager and team act in a professional and ethical manner?

1115. What function(s) does it fill or meet?

1116. Does it do what client said it would?

1117. Did the Architecture Competency project achieve its MOV?

1118. What lessons were learned about your Architecture Competency project management methodology?

1119. What can you do better next time?

1120. How well did the team follow the methodology?

1121. Do you buy pre-configured systems or build your own configuration?

1122. What is the Acceptance Management Process?

1123. Does it do what Architecture Competency project team said it would?

1124. Who supplies data?

1125. Do you buy-in installation services?

1126. What was done right?

1127. Was business value realized?

5.0 Closing Process Group: Architecture Competency

1128. Were cost budgets met?

1129. If action is called for, what form should it take?

1130. What is the Architecture Competency project name and date of completion?

1131. Did you do things well?

1132. Just how important is your work to the overall success of the Architecture Competency project?

1133. Were the outcomes different from the already stated planned?

1134. What do you need to do?

1135. What areas does the group agree are the biggest success on the Architecture Competency project?

1136. What was learned?

1137. What can you do better next time, and what specific actions can you take to improve?

1138. Did the Architecture Competency project team have enough people to execute the Architecture Competency project plan?

1139. How well did the chosen processes fit the needs of the Architecture Competency project?

1140. How will staff learn how to use the deliverables?

1141. How critical is the Architecture Competency project success to the success of your organization?

1142. Does the close educate others to improve performance?

1143. Is this an updated Architecture Competency project Proposal Document?

1144. How will you know you did it?

5.1 Procurement Audit: Architecture Competency

1145. Are signature plates under the control of someone other than the individual given check-signing accountability?

1146. Are petty cash funds operated on an imprest basis?

1147. Was the outcome of the award process properly reached and communicated?

1148. Do the employees have the necessary skills and experience to carry out procurements efficiently?

1149. Were technical requirements set strict enough to guarantee the desired performance without being unnecessarily tight to exclude favourable bids that do not comply with all requirements?

1150. Are all initial purchase contracts made by the purchasing organization?

1151. If an order is divided among several vendors, is the explanation for that procedure documented?

1152. Has management taken the necessary steps to ensure that relevant control systems are always up to date?

1153. Have late payment interests been rewarded and could they have been avoided?

1154. Are there mechanisms in place to evaluate the performance of the departments suppliers?

1155. Does your organization use existing contracts where possible to avoid the cost of bidding?

1156. Was the estimated contract value in line with the final cost of the contract awarded?

1157. Has the department identified and described the different elements in the procurement process?

1158. Are buyers prohibited from accepting gifts from vendors?

1159. Is there any objection?

1160. Are the pages of the minutes book press pre-numbered?

1161. Does the strategy ensure that the best supplier is chosen considering: price, quality, service, dependable operation, internal operation costs, life time operation costs and codes of ethic?

1162. Does the procurement function/unit have the ability to apply public procurement principles and to prepare tender and contract documents?

1163. Are controls proportionated to risks?

1164. Is the appropriate procurement approach being chosen (considering for example the possibility of contracting out work or procuring low value items through a specific low cost procuring system)?

5.2 Contract Close-Out: Architecture Competency

1165. Parties: who is involved?

1166. Change in knowledge?

1167. Was the contract sufficiently clear so as not to result in numerous disputes and misunderstandings?

1168. Why Outsource?

1169. How is the contracting office notified of the automatic contract close-out?

1170. What happens to the recipient of services?

1171. How/when used ?

1172. Parties: Authorized?

1173. Are the signers the authorized officials?

1174. Have all acceptance criteria been met prior to final payment to contractors?

1175. What is capture management?

1176. Have all contract records been included in the Architecture Competency project archives?

1177. Have all contracts been completed?

1178. Was the contract type appropriate?

1179. Has each contract been audited to verify acceptance and delivery?

1180. Was the contract complete without requiring numerous changes and revisions?

1181. Change in attitude or behavior?

1182. Change in circumstances?

1183. How does it work?

1184. Have all contracts been closed?

5.3 Project or Phase Close-Out: Architecture Competency

1185. Did the Architecture Competency project management methodology work?

1186. Were risks identified and mitigated?

1187. What were the goals and objectives of the communications strategy for the Architecture Competency project?

1188. What benefits or impacts does the stakeholder group expect to obtain as a result of the Architecture Competency project?

1189. Who controlled key decisions that were made?

1190. What information is each stakeholder group interested in?

1191. What process was planned for managing issues/ risks?

1192. What are the informational communication needs for each stakeholder?

1193. Did the delivered product meet the specified requirements and goals of the Architecture Competency project?

1194. Does the lesson educate others to improve performance?

1195. Who exerted influence that has positively affected or negatively impacted the Architecture Competency project?

1196. What could be done to improve the process?

1197. What were the actual outcomes?

1198. How often did each stakeholder need an update?

1199. In addition to assessing whether the Architecture Competency project was successful, it is equally critical to analyze why it was or was not fully successful. Are you including this?

1200. How much influence did the stakeholder have over others?

1201. What was expected from each stakeholder?

1202. Who is responsible for award close-out?

1203. What is a Risk?

5.4 Lessons Learned: Architecture Competency

1204. What skills did you need that were missing on this Architecture Competency project?

1205. What are the internal dependencies?

1206. Are the lessons more complex and multivariate?

1207. How timely was the training you received in preparation for the use of the product/service?

1208. What regulatory regime controlled how your organization head and program manager directed your organization and Architecture Competency project?

1209. What is the supervisor to staff ratio?

1210. Who has execution authority?

1211. How efficient is the deliverable?

1212. What is the impact of tax policy on the case?

1213. What is the desired end-state?

1214. Is the lesson significant, valid, and applicable?

1215. What is the expected lifespan of the deliverable?

1216. How effective were your design reviews?

1217. How effective were the techniques used to prepare you and your organization for the impact of the changes brought about by the product or service produced by the Architecture Competency project?

1218. What is your working hypothesis, if you have one?

1219. What would you approach differently next time?

1220. Are new goals needed?

1221. How was the Architecture Competency project controlled?

1222. Did the Architecture Competency project management methodology work?

1223. What worked well/did not work well?

Index

delivery   23, 56, 111, 118, 165, 259
Delphi 219
demand   117, 204
demands   242-243
department   8, 106, 197, 221, 257
depend   220
dependable   257
dependent   118, 134, 144
depends   111
deploy 97, 126
deployed   96, 144
deploying   47
deployment   53
derive 100, 165
Describe   19, 148, 152, 166, 215, 222, 250-251
described   1, 151, 184, 200, 224, 257
describing   40
deserving   221
design 1, 10, 64, 69, 76, 78, 97, 122, 156, 186, 215, 262
designated   159
designed   8, 10, 62, 75, 81, 90
designing   8
desired24, 41, 62, 80, 224, 237, 246, 256, 262
detail   56, 80, 151, 154, 206, 222
detailed   71-72, 131, 138, 145, 157, 193
details 44
detect 95
determine   10, 108, 123, 139, 161, 172, 182, 187, 211
determined   70, 108, 133, 190-191, 201
determines   180
detracting   119
develop   55, 75, 79, 86, 144, 154, 215
developed   10, 29, 31-32, 45, 77, 84, 142, 159-161, 172, 190,
216, 219, 225, 246, 248
developers   206
developing   69, 78, 212
devices   233
diagram   3, 50, 53, 67, 167, 177
diagrams   57, 196
Dictionary   3, 156
difference   138, 159, 176, 219, 226
different   8, 24, 29, 32, 41, 61, 67, 108, 122, 139-140, 153,
204, 227, 254, 257

importance   235, 243
important   17, 22, 41, 60, 62, 109-110, 115-116, 120, 139, 145,
185, 189, 219, 234-235, 248, 254
imprest 256
improve   2, 10, 65, 75-76, 78-79, 84-86, 88-90, 131, 133-134,
170, 188, 230, 254-255, 260-261
improved   77, 85, 89, 95, 228
improves   131
improving   84, 220
inactive   180
incentives   94
include   23, 88, 150, 162, 179
included   2, 8, 17, 52, 146, 151, 174-175, 183, 222, 250-251,
258
INCLUDES   10
including   25, 37, 39, 41, 47, 73, 87, 95, 102, 153, 157, 160,
261
increase   76, 127
increased   110
increasing   117
incurred   45
incurring   156
in-depth   9, 11
indicate   65, 94, 115
indicated   100
indicators   16, 49, 55, 60, 68, 71, 78, 156, 205
indirect   53, 156, 180, 192, 245
indirectly   1
individual   1, 49, 161, 194, 233, 235, 242-243, 250, 256
industrial   207
industry   100, 119, 123, 142, 166
infinite 125
influence   78, 116, 135, 139, 226, 236, 261
influences   165, 239
informal   242-243
informed   124, 132, 192
ingrained   98
inherent   125
in-house   134
initial   33, 107, 256
initially 34
initiated   182, 224
Initiating   2, 113, 131

286